Mastering the Piano

MERVYN BRUXNER

Mastering the Piano

A GUIDE FOR THE AMATEUR

FABER AND FABER
3 Queen Square
London

First published in 1972
by Faber & Faber Limited
3 Queen Square London WC1
Printed in Great Britain by
Latimer Trend & Co Ltd Plymouth
All rights reserved

ISBN 0 571 09629 8

To Salene

Contents

9

Preface

If you are an amateur pianist who would like to be able to play better than you can at present, but have little time, then this book is aimed at you.

It would be better if you are not much younger than seventeen, because if you are, you should be having individual lessons, and not much older than seventy, because after that age, it is harder to change one's habits and accept new ideas—though some septuagenarians can do both.

Of course, it is a great advantage to have lessons, whatever age you are, but there are some advantages in learning from a book. As an author I cannot tell what your peculiar physical or temperamental difficulties may be, as I might be able to find out if I were in a room teaching you, but in some ways it is much better that I should not be able to look over your shoulder all the time, and better that you should not continually turn round and ask questions. It has been said that all education is self-education; and I am convinced you *can* teach yourself with a little guidance. Indeed, even if you were to have lessons, you should still try to teach yourself more than any teacher could teach you.

The right way to learn a particular point is to absorb the general principles and then find out how far and in what ways you can apply them yourself. In this book I shall try to explain some of the general principles, so far as I have learned them from the patient people who taught me, and then I shall urge you to apply them to your own playing and to find out yourself, when you get to some difficulty, just what the problem is for you and how you can overcome it. To help you to

11

Preface

do this, I have included comments on particular and common difficulties in a number of mostly well-known pieces of piano music.

There are two good reasons why it is worth while reviving and improving your piano-playing. The first is to play pleasurably to yourself; the second, to play with other people, either as an accompanist or as one of an ensemble—a thing that too few amateur pianists think of doing. To play to oneself is not necessarily a selfish thing to do, nor is it the same kind of thing as the professional pianist does when he plays to an audience. Every musical person wants to make music, to express himself; and if the piano is your instrument, why should you not use it for your own pleasure? There are thousands of excellent piano pieces within the reach of the amateur who has no ambition to emulate the great players.

To play with other people is most rewarding and a great stimulus. To accompany a singer or instrumentalist, or to play the piano part of a violin sonata or piano trio or quartet, is even more exciting. All pianists should explore these possibilities. And if you ever do play to an audience it is far less nerve-racking than playing alone.

Three people have kindly read this book in typescript and made valuable suggestions for its improvement: Miss Mary Ibberson, Miss Yvonne Enoch and Mr. Herbert Shead. I acknowledge with much gratitude the help which they have given me.

M. B.

CHAPTER 1

Basic Essentials

There are some qualities of mind and body which you must have if you want to play the piano pleasurably: there are other qualities which you must acquire and develop as you study the instrument. Let us begin with those you need at the start.

1. You must want to play the piano

If you do not want to play, you will of course not have read as far as this. But if you do want to play, even if you know that you may never play very well and not nearly as well as a professional pianist, then I should like to help you. I am sure that you would rather play by yourself than to anybody: the day has long passed when amateur pianists could entertain their friends and relatives by bringing their 'piece' to a party. Nowadays we can all hear the same piece much better played on a record. But one can get much pleasure out of playing to oneself. It is a different kind of pleasure from that of listening to a good pianist on a record or broadcast. You play to yourself not only to listen, but to express yourself; and you do this because every musical person wants to express emotion through sounds, through making music, even if the results are imperfect. Besides, the very difficulty of playing and the excitement of overcoming the difficulty have a value of their own to you.

I do not think, however, that it is much good having merely a general motive for improvement. Every musician wishes he were a better player of something, and would like to play better 'some day'. Such a motive may be admirable, but it is usually ineffective. It is far better to have an immediate and more

13

specific reason for wanting to play well: a concert next week, or a meeting with a good player of some other instrument who wants you to accompany him.

2. You must be prepared to spend some time regularly practising

Or in thinking what you will do when you do practise. For some suggestions about practising, see Chapter Two.

3. You must be reasonably well-equipped physically

(a) Your hand-stretch from thumb to little finger on each hand should extend to at least an octave. If it does not, you may have to confine yourself to music which requires only small stretches.

(b) *You must be able to move your arms up and down and sideways*, your hands in the same way, your forearms clockwise and anti-clockwise, and your fingers independently of each other, though it does not matter if neighbouring fingers affect each other's movements.

(c) *Your sight must be good enough* for you to read music easily as you sit at the piano. I only mention this because I know some players who are unaware of having slightly defective sight and do not wear glasses when they should.

(d) *Your ear must be able to recognize differences of pitch.*

(e) *You must be able to remember* in outline the sounds of music which you have played or heard frequently.

(f) *You must be prepared to be systematic*, however unsystematic you may be by nature. You cannot know how much time and trouble you can save yourself by a modicum of system until you have tried.

No doubt there are other qualities necessary for pianists, but you can discover them for yourself and add them to my list. Let us now consider what characteristics you must acquire and develop. I assume that you already understand musical notation.

Basic Essentials

A. *A geographical sense of the keyboard, by touch*
I rate this very high among your priorities. If you cannot find your way about the keyboard without looking at your hands all the time, you will never play fluently and you will always be a bad sight-reader. There are no exceptions to this dogmatic statement.

B. *Technical competence*
This is a huge subject on which many books have been written. Here I shall try to describe only the basic principles. It will then be for you to develop, as much as you can, your abilities within those principles. Naturally the professional pianist must develop his technique to a high degree, but the amateur can get a great deal of pleasure out of piano-playing without having what the newspapers call a 'dazzling' technique. If you work *with* the natural tendencies of your limbs and muscles and not, as many people do, against them, you give yourself a chance of improving your technique—and therefore your pleasure—many times over.

C. *Memorizing*
By memorizing I mean not only to retain sounds in your head but to remember at least some of the notes which make those sounds. If you know the tune of the national anthem, for instance, it is most useful to know that the notes G, G, A, F sharp, G and A make its first phrase. There are, of course, many other things that contribute to a musical memory, such as muscular memory, knowledge of harmony and design. We shall be discussing these later.

D. *Rhythm*
The word rhythm has been the most misused and the most misinterpreted of all words used to describe music. It has been given too many different meanings. But since it is the very life-blood of music, every pianist—every musician, come to that—must

15

understand the constituents of rhythm, feel it in his bones and show it in his playing.

The first constituent of rhythm is the beat. The beat, or pulse if you like, permeates nearly all music and, once established, goes on remorselessly through a piece until the composer directs some alteration of it. This beat is not in itself rhythm, but only the basis of it; and any irregularity of speed becomes significant only in relation to the regularity of the beat. The pianist does not necessarily play the beat all the time, but he must feel it all the time.

The next constituent of rhythm is 'time'. I put this word in quote marks because it is a technical term in music. It means the division of the pulse-like beat into regular stresses and non-stresses. As you know very well, this is normally done by dividing music into 'bars' in each of which there is a definite number of beats; and it is a convention that the first beat of a bar is a little more stressed than the others in the same bar, and the last beat in a bar less stressed. Of course there are many occasions when this convention is deliberately ignored or avoided. But since human beings enjoy both convention and the breaking of it, they enjoy both regular stresses such as one gets, for example, in 'three in a bar' where every third beat is stressed, mixed up with occasional moments of irregular stresses caused by tied notes, rests and so on. But of course irregularity is fun only where there is regularity to compare it with, just as the school-boy enjoys breaking a rule because there is a rule to break.

Several consecutive bars may all have a regular beat behind them, but each bar may have a different 'rhythm', because the notes (in their time sense) may not coincide with the beat. In some simple music, such as military marches, there may occasionally be stretches of music in which the notes and the beats coincide. Notes, however, must be related in the player's mind to a beat; and he must know exactly what relationship each note has to the beat, whether it is a fraction of it, identical with it, or a multiple of it.

Finally there exists rhythm in the wider sense: a group of

bars may correspond rhythmically with another group of bars, just as a line of verse may correspond with another (not necessarily the next) line of verse. Musicians talk of 'bar rhythm' in these cases. Usually these groups consist of a fairly small number of bars and it is quite easy to feel their rhythm. But occasionally the scale of operations is much larger. Tovey, the great critic, pointed out that the first *Kyrie* of Bach's B Minor Mass, which has a fugue of over a hundred bars in length, ends punctually!

The following examples may make clear some of these complexities:

Example 1

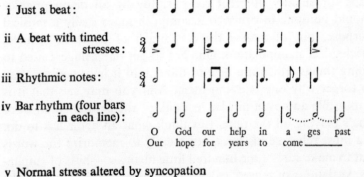

i Just a beat:

ii A beat with timed stresses:

iii Rhythmic notes:

iv Bar rhythm (four bars in each line):

O God our help in a - ges past
Our hope for years to come

v Normal stress altered by syncopation

Allegro molto vivace   Beethoven Op. 21

cresc.   *sf*   *sf*

E. *Imaginative listening*
Perhaps I can best explain what I mean by this by giving you an example of its opposite. A short time ago I went to a concert given by an amateur orchestra of some merit. I enjoyed some of the concert very much, but one piece—by Haydn, I think—required the cellos and basses to play the note D about thirty-two times running with only an occasional A here and there. My ears got stuck on to that note D and I could hear nothing

else. Of course it was Haydn's doing, not the orchestra's, that this note came so often, but I'm afraid that it was the players who made it sound monotonous and so little connected with what the rest of the orchestra was doing. The cellos just sat there and played their pom-pom-pom-pom crotchets thirty-two times without any variation at all. Of course I know that all these crotchets on the same note are not in themselves a great stimulus to inspired playing, but there was a nice tune above them. I felt that those poor cellists could have listened to that tune and fitted their humdrum crotchets to it with some regard to its phrasing and general shape. The cellists were not unmusical. They were just not listening imaginatively.

The same kind of thing can happen to pianists, though perhaps for slightly different reasons. Ideally all piano practice should be done in order to accomplish more easily a musical purpose, but of course there is much of it which requires mechanical manipulation. One has to get one's fingers used to doing things which are new to them, and it is sometimes easy to forget why one is doing them. And you may say that it is impossible and even unwise to think of the emotional effect of one's playing all the time. But think what an actor has to do. He must rehearse his lines, not merely to memorize the words but to make sure of the hundred little nuances—shifts of emphasis, variations of tempo, calculated silences—which go to make up an intelligent performance. He has to practise all these things over and over again until he is sure that he can do them all without hesitation; and it may be that some of them will become stereotyped and mechanical. Indeed, a bad actor may easily become a 'hack' without noticing it. But the good actor will be sensitive to the occasion, and nothing he says will be absolutely frozen and identical with the way he did it before. He will always leave scope for a little variety. And, come the first night with all its uncertainty and excitement, the rehearsed emotions of each sentence will become not only merged with those of the whole play, but will also receive something back from the audience and will be revived in the process. A musician is in the same position. Even if much of his practising has been mechanical, if he has formed the habit of listening imaginatively both to his own playing and, even more, to the playing of anyone working with him, all these mechanics will come alive in performance.

The bad pianist will 'rattle through' a familiar piece, not bothering about the unremarkable phrases, but the good one will make every phrase significant, because it is part of the whole piece. Listen to a good recording of the playing of Claudio Arrau, or any other great artist, and you will find yourself attending all the time. He has made every phrase significant. His concentration has compelled yours.

F. *Playing music of a past age*
How far should one adhere to the styles of past generations? Some purists believe that one should perform Bach, for example, exactly as Bach himself would have performed his own works in the eighteenth century. That is a point of view both reasonable and valuable, for we must all surely benefit by finding out what sort of sounds Bach had in mind when he wrote his music. So one of your jobs as a pianist is to learn something about past generations of musicians and the conditions in which they worked, and the instruments they used.

On the other hand there is some justification for performing the music of the past in a manner coloured by the times one lives in, and in many ways it is unavoidable. Both our instruments and our musical experiences are different from those of Bach's time. So, although I believe one should pay much heed to history and avoid doing things plainly contrary to the spirit of an 'old' composer when you perform his music, I do not raise hands in horror when music written for a harpsichord is played on a piano, nor even when I hear Bach 'swingled' or jazzed up, provided it is done with skill and artistic feeling.

G. *How the Piano works*
I do not myself set so much store on this knowledge as some

19

people do, perhaps because I am not mechanically minded. We all have to use or control so many machines nowadays, whose workings are complex, that it does not seem to me to matter greatly if we do not know all about their 'innards'. But obviously it is a good thing for anyone who plays the piano to know roughly how it works: the shape of the keyboard* (which you think you know, but probably don't—try to draw a diagram of it without looking at a piano), how the pedals work, and what happens to the hammer when you put down a key. Most of these things can be found out simply by taking off the lid or the front of the instrument and looking inside.

A pianist is unfortunate in that he cannot, as a violinist can, take his instrument about with him and treat it almost as part of himself. But if you have a reasonably good piano at home, treat it as a friend and take care of it. Listen to its sounds with affection, and persuade it rather than command it to do what you want.

* The note G, for example, is not in quite the same spatial relationship to G sharp as F is to F sharp.

CHAPTER 2

Practising

The object of practising an instrument is to learn as quickly as possible how to play something on it. If you are a child when you start, your parents hope that one day you will be able to play the piano well, even if that day is years ahead. But the child does not think years ahead, he wants to play a piece now, tomorrow or next week. So, I expect, do you. Perhaps you have a little more patience than a child, but you want to learn *quickly*. I think you are right. You should do all you can to learn quickly.

The best and most effective motive for learning a piece of music is to give yourself pleasure. You have heard a piece somewhere, you have liked it very much and you yearn to play it yourself. That is good, but the only snag is that it may be such a difficult piece that you cannot play it for a very long time. So do not be too ambitious at first: it is better to play a fairly easy piece well than to make a hash of Tchaikovsky's celebrated Concerto in B flat minor. The moment you realize that you have done something well, you feel more confident. The next piece will not seem so hard.

All the time you play you should be trying to make the music sound as you want it. You must do this on purpose. It is no good thinking the thing will 'come right' in the end on its own. It is very difficult to keep the searchlight of your critical faculty focused on your own playing, but all the time you must be self-critical and say to yourself: 'is it sounding as I want it to sound?' All the great artists are humble people, because they have learned to criticize themselves.

Do not despise routine. Routine is a great ally. If you settle

21

definite days and times for practice, stick to them if you possibly can, because routine helps you. Your physical digestion works better if your meals are at regular times, your mental and emotional digestion does too. Do not skip a practice because you do not feel like it, unless you are really ill. Often the practice itself will make you 'feel like it'. In fact, almost every practice needs a warming-up period of mind and body.

For how long should one practise? I cannot answer that because I do not know your circumstances. Short regular practices often are more valuable than long, infrequent sessions. You cannot achieve much in less than half·an hour because, as I said, you need a quarter of an hour for 'warming up'. On the other hand it is useless to go on practising when you are very tired or when you continually have to pull your attention back to what you are doing.

GOLDEN RULE No. 1. Practise with the aim of never making a mistake

Every time you make a mistake you are more likely to make it again. Every time you manage to play a tricky passage without blemish, it will be a little bit easier to do so next time. Of course, 'never make a mistake' is a counsel of perfection, and there are some kinds of practice, as when you do arm movements for the sake of getting used to the movements, when you needn't bother about the right notes at all. Otherwise, the nearer you can get to the 'no mistakes' ideal, the better. This leads to:

GOLDEN RULE No. 2. Learn how to practise slowly

Much of your practice will be to make your brain and fingers do unfamiliar things, so you must get used to exercises by degrees. Besides, you will practise more intelligently and easily if you do not feel hurried at first. Don't forget that your brain comes first. Make sure that you get your thoughts straight before you ask your fingers to do something. People who complain that a piece of music never 'comes right' are blaming the piece when they should blame themselves.

But naturally you must learn too how to play something up to speed, and often speed itself is the difficulty. You can learn how to go from slow to fast by playing fast for very small stretches of time, then pausing or playing slowly again, and finally another burst of speed. The brain can take in, and act rapidly on very short bits of information. You could probably remember and repeat quickly someone's telephone number of only four or five figures, but you might find eight or nine figures difficult, if the whole sequence was new to you.

GOLDEN RULE No. 3. Be easy in mind and body
Another counsel of perfection? Of course! But absolutely vital to your progress. The greatest enemy of the practising pianist is *Fear*, fear of messing up an unfamiliar movement, fear of playing a wrong note, fear of being unable to combine two different movements, one in each hand. I am not now talking about the fear of playing in public but of the fear, often partly unconscious, which assails you when you are alone. Any sense of struggle, any gritting of teeth, stiffening of muscles or even holding of the breath—any of these may be a warning sign that you are scared stiff.

Mind and body interact all the time. If you sit easily and move smoothly you are more likely to think clearly and without anxiety. Conversely, if you think clearly and happily, you are more likely to move easily. I shall have more to say about this in the chapter on Technique (see pages 33, 48) later. Meanwhile, remember that you can practise positive things, like thinking clearly and sitting easily and moving your hands and arms and fingers smoothly, which make fear less likely to conquer you. If you try this out and find that it helps, then do it every time, not just on Tuesdays in Lent.

There is one most annoying thing about practising—that it is not performing. To practise properly one continually has to stop, repeat something and break the continuity of the music. Many people never really practise properly for that single reason, they cannot bear to stop! I think that the only remedy is to decide at the start that practising is a business-like, largely mechanical process during which you are learning to do certain specific things with your brain and fingers. You will not, of course, always start at the beginning of a piece—you can play that bit—but at the difficult part which defeated you last time. When you come to a difficulty you will stop and discover exactly what the difficulty is. That is not always easy to do or even to try to do. You hear a wrong note or a muffed phrase and all you can think of is, I must try that bit again. But it is no use trying it again unless you know what it is you are trying to do that you didn't do before, to make the thing sound right. In other words, you have got to think out for yourself what your hands are doing wrong and why.

Of course, there comes a time with every piece of learning when you want to see, or rather hear, the piece as a whole and to play it through without stopping. Or it may be that the first half is worth playing through in that way. It is helpful to do this and it represents another stage of practising, a stage beyond the mere mechanics of technique and a stage nearer to the music itself. Strangely enough, this 'play-through' can make one quite nervous, even if one is alone in the room. And a good thing too, I say; because one has to get used to this sense of occasion. Practising alone as if there really were an audience is a necessary preparation to playing when there is one.

This book is not intended primarily for the player in public, but every amateur may be inveigled into playing to an audience and will usually be in a horrible state of fright beforehand. How does one get over concert nerves? It is very hard for the occasional performer in public to overcome them, because one of the ways of doing it is, of course, to perform often. But the main remedy for fright is to know for certain that you can do what you are trying to do. If, for instance, I had to recite the even numbers up to twenty to an audience of eight thousand at the Albert Hall—an unlikely contingency—I know I could do it. I should probably feel a bit scared at the prospect of just standing in such a conspicuous position before eight thousand people, but I know I could say those numbers. I shouldn't be so scared as to forget them. In the same way, if you *know* that you can play your piece without difficulty, you will be scared perhaps—and I think one should be scared, it tones you up no end—but you will not be so frightened as to be paralysed. You will certainly not play it worse than usual. And if you really know your job, you will play it better.

Most people who seldom play to an audience think of it as a hostile body of people sitting out there in the hall waiting for the appearance of some unfortunate pianist so as to tear him to pieces. But of course, part of the job of the artist is to make friends with his audience. Watch any television comedian and you'll see it happen. So if you have to play in public, especially if it is a public in which some of your friends are lurking, which somehow makes it much worse, try to make real friends with them somehow. If it is not too formal an occasion it would be a good thing to talk to the audience for a minute about the piece or pieces you are going to play, talking in an informal and friendly way and above all naturally, as if you want them to enjoy themselves and feel pretty sure that they will. And if you are in an audience which has to welcome a nervous performer, give him a big hand before he has begun, to encourage him. You may not feel like doing it afterwards!

You can practise a piece, as I have already implied, in several different ways. You can select passages of particular difficulty and learn how to solve their technical problems, you can concentrate on memorizing or on general interpretative mastery. Part of the time at least may be spent on thinking about the music, without actually playing it. So practice need never be dull. You can always vary your approach if one line of attack tends to pall. But stick to one thing at a time, until you are sure that you are making no headway, and try to improve in at least one way before you stop, so that you can leave the piano with a sense of achievement, however small. If you have honestly tried hard to conquer any particular difficulty and think you have failed, do not flog yourself beyond the point of calm repetition. Leave it alone, and next day you may find it has solved itself. What has really happened is that the unconscious mind, which plays such a large part in small, skilled actions, has gone on where you consciously left off.

A very common fate overtakes some conscientious pianists: they practise something so often that it gets worse instead of better, and if they begin thinking about a passage that has been played automatically, they get worse still. You may have heard of the centipede who was asked which leg he was going to put forward next. He was so confused that he couldn't move at all! This sometimes happens to the pianist for the same reason; thoughtless, mechanical practice. The old-fashioned books of technical exercises sometimes contained the direction: 'play this twenty times', and the luckless student just played it twenty times without any thought in his head except to count the number of times he played it. One student actually kept a stack of cards, twenty in number, on the left of the music-stand and transferred one card to the right-hand side after each playing of the passage until all twenty cards had been used up. He then stopped and congratulated himself on a marvellous practice.

But of course, this is all wrong. Such practice always leads to disaster because the player has allowed his fingers automatic self-government. I am not saying that automatic finger-memory is useless: on the contrary, it is most helpful and necessary. But it should never be your main memory, for it is a good servant and a bad master. If you allow your fingers to rule you, they will let you down. They have no sense of public decency. What you must do is to always maintain a general control of your fingers from the brain. This brain-control may itself become almost automatic, but it *is* control. Your fingers by themselves are un-controlled. Let me explain once more by the familiar analogy of numbers. You can, of course, count up to five; your tongue could say 'one-two-three-four-five' quickly and automatically.

Practising

You could probably say it in your sleep. But somewhere inside your head there is, believe it or not, a brain which knows all about one-two-three-four-five; knows what it means and which is the right order of the numbers. If a flash of lightning occurred while you were counting and had already said 'one-two-three', you could stop and add on 'four-five' afterwards when you remembered that it was only the local electrician testing your lighting system again. In the same way you can keep a kind of mental-aural control of your finger movements. The 'think' may be so easy and quick as to be almost automatic, but it is still a 'think' and in control of your fingers. If you can stop a quick finger passage in the middle and then go on and finish it, then you are in command of it.

GOLDEN RULE No. 4. Thinking and Listening are the most important parts of practising
You think what sort of sound you want, before you have made it; then you listen as you make it to discover whether it was what you wanted. If not, as we shall see in later chapters, you think again to discover the reason.

One more point about practising: rhythm. I have talked in the previous chapter about the onward-moving momentum of music. I now want to remind you of the importance of ordinary, metrical rhythm of, say, four beats to a bar. This feeling of pulse—for that is what it really is—must permeate all your practising. If you are one of those people who are a bit weak on 'time' and do not worry very much how long a dotted crotchet is in a particular context, then I must tell you straight away that you will never be much good as a pianist until you have taken steps to improve yourself in this respect. But if you do take the trouble, then I can promise you that all your playing will eventually sound better and, what is more, all your practising will be more fun. For this underlying pulse is like petrol to a car: it makes it go! And you must see to it that you never are without it.

Practising

In the early stages of pulse-learning, it is as well to beat time, perhaps with your foot, and religiously fit every single note and dotted note and rest into that beat. If you are not used to this, you may find it irksome at first, but only for a short time: and ever afterwards you will be urged on by the pulse. If, on the other hand, you are a good time keeper you need not actually beat time, but you must have it in your head all the way and you can then afford to let the pulse go a little faster or a little slower in places where the music needs it.

'Ha-ha! Keep time,' said Shakespeare's Richard II. 'How sour sweet music is when time is broke and no proportion kept.'

CHAPTER 3

Technique (1):
The Geography of the Keyboard

I suggested earlier that you should become one with your instrument. An early stage in this courtship, as in most other courtships, is to find your way about with your fingers, enjoying the tactile sense of feeling the keys and discovering your way about by sense of touch, not by your sense of sight. Very many amateur pianists have become despondent simply because they have never realized the importance of this tactile skill, or if they have realized it, have done nothing about it.

If you think for a moment, you can easily see what is wrong about finding notes on a piano merely by looking for them with your eyes. Your eyes have too much else to do. You cannot very well look at your right hand, your left hand, and the music simultaneously, because your eyes cannot look in three different directions at once. You can sometimes see more than one thing at a time, but only if they are all in the same direction. By the time you have looked at your left hand, your right hand, the music and then again at your hands, you will have lost the place probably in all three directions. Many a poor pianist has suffered from this, and has usually given up all hope of playing the piano in consequence. And if you still have any doubts about the wise way of doing things, which is, of course, to *look* at the music and *feel* your way about on the keyboard with your hands, think what other instrumentalists do. The violinist does not look at his fingers to see where to put them on the string, nor the flautist at the holes in his flute. And ask any good typist how she learned to 'play' the typewriter.

29

Technique (1) The Geography of the Keyboard

At this point you might want to say to me that you have watched many famous pianists play and that they all looked at their hands, so why shouldn't you? The answer is that the professional solo pianist leads quite a different sort of life and has quite a different set of objectives from those of the amateur. He has to memorize a large repertoire well enough to play confidently in public; the amateur plays only seldom in public, but would like to be able to play to himself and to play informally as an accompanist or partner to other people. He is most useful as a good sight-reader of music, while the professional soloist seldom has to read anything at sight in front of anyone else. Besides, he has already gone through the 'geography-of-the-keyboard' stage; and now he can look at his hands as much as he likes. So could you. Once your hands have learned their way about the keyboard, they will never forget it.

I am as certain as I am of anything that you will never be even a moderately fluent sight-reader at the piano until you have learned to play without looking at your hands. But of course, there is much more to it than just sight-reading. You cannot really be a fluent pianist at all, even of memorized music, unless you can play by sense of touch, any more than a driver of a car can drive easily and safely if he cannot use his gear-handle, his clutch or his brakes without looking at them.

Let us see what is involved in learning what I have called the 'geography' of the keyboard.

1. *Posture and Balance.* Since you cannot go anywhere without knowing where you start from, you must consistently sit on your piano stool in the same spatial relation to the keyboard every time, and you must sit so that you can move your arms and hands and fingers easily to find and play the notes.

2. *Distance-judging.* This means judging *by feel* the distance between notes on the keyboard that are (a) next door to each other, (b) next door but playable with other than next-door fingers, (c) a short distance apart, and (d) far enough apart to involve a new hand position.

1. POSTURE AND BALANCE

Sit bang opposite the middle of the keyboard, with the lock of the keyboard lid opposite the middle of your tummy. This will bring you opposite the notes E or F immediately above Middle C. Middle C itself is not in the middle of the keyboard, it is only called 'middle' because it is halfway between the printed bass and treble clefs.

You should sit close enough to the keyboard so as to be able to play simultaneously the top and bottom notes of the piano with each of your fifth fingers, but not so close that it is uncomfortable for your two hands to approach each other in front of you until your two thumbs touch. I have, myself, long arms and can easily reach the extreme notes at top or bottom, but if you have short arms there is nothing wrong in leaning forward a little for the extreme notes and a little back for the near ones.

The main principle for all posture is that your arms should feel as free to move as possible. Keep your elbows two or three inches away from the sides of your body, and do not be afraid to move the body a little to help any position of the arms. You must, of course, sit firmly on the stool, preferably not too far back on it, but forward enough to give you freedom of movement.

Another principle of equal importance is that all your movements of arms or hands, or even fingers, should be the result of a balanced body. Think of every movement as if made by a cat, smooth and lithe and timed, because your body itself is balanced and comfortable. Put your feet out in front of you with the heels on the ground and quite close to each other, so that the ball of either foot can depress its appropriate pedal easily. You should feel that your whole body is comfortably balanced, the weight of your body on the seat, the weight of your legs on the ground under your heels. Balance is not a static state, it implies potential movement. You should feel able to move your body forward or backward, or side to side freely and easily; and to move your arms and hands without difficulty and without disturbing your basic balance. In the same way, if you want to make balanced and controlled movements with your forearms, your upper arm and elbow must be firm.

One of the difficulties of learning or teaching piano technique is that much that concerns posture and balance is invisible. Many movements, too, are so small as to be hardly noticeable from outside. I can make all these suggestions about the positions of your body, arms and legs; but they will be of no use to you until you yourself *feel* them to be right. So it is infinitely worth while for you to start every practice with a deliberate posture-and-balance thought and experiment, and even to re-think and re-experiment in the middle of a practice, especially when you feel that the difficulty of the piece you are practising is getting you down. There is a particularly satisfying sensation about being physically balanced. Your body should be balanced on the fulcrum of your hips, your arms on the shoulders, your forearms on the elbows, your hands on your wrists and even your fingers from each knuckle. You can think separately about any of these limbs, but in practice they all depend on each other. You cannot be really happy about the movement of a finger unless your whole body is balanced.

It is most important that you should adopt, after trial and perhaps error, the posture and balance which suits you. So if anything you have read here or elsewhere, or anything you have been told, conflicts with what you feel to be right for you, then adopt your own way of doing something. The wise man will listen to advice from informed people, but in the end he will make up his own mind what to do, even if it is against some expert's view. Never do what someone else says you should do, unless you are in some disciplined situation or unless you have considered his advice and agree with it. Half the foolish, gormless people of this world are foolish and gormless because they rely entirely on other people's brains and ideas and never think for themselves.

The purpose of balanced posture and movements is to make

skilled movement possible and easy. Ask any boxer, cricketer, footballer or tennis player, and look at any member of the cat tribe. A balanced body is also, I believe, half-way to having a balanced mind. You know how coroners' juries talk of people who have committed suicide as having done so 'while the balance of their mind was disturbed', meaning that they were not quite sane. I would never dream of suggesting that my despondent pianist was as bad as that, but there is no doubt that he can get mentally twisted up in knots by the various difficulties of piano-playing; and that often leads to his getting twisted up physically.

I used, at one time, to have lessons from a most generous and capable lady who gave me lessons for a very small fee, just because she liked teaching. One day, after talking about some other things, she complained of my inattention. This surprised and upset me a little, as I thought I was drinking in every word she said. I was in a glum mood for quite a time, until I realized from some further discussion of technique that what she had really complained about was not my inattention but my inner tension! I was so anxious to please her and so anxious to improve that my mind was in a continuous state of tense worry, for fear that I should play badly; and consequently my hands and arms and fingers were unduly tensed too. I shall have more to say about 'inner tension' in a later chapter. Remember that the beginning of ease of playing is how you sit.

2. DISTANCE-JUDGING

Hundreds of years ago, the builders of organ keyboards made each note so big that you had to use your whole fist to play one. Since then, the makers of keyboard instruments have become less expansive and have made notes to fit the fingers. If you put your right thumb on, say, G above middle C, it is quite easy to play the next note above, A, with the second finger, B with the third finger and so on. Try and do this with your eyes shut (after finding the first G) and you will have taken the first

c

step towards fluent playing. Everybody's hand is, of course, different, but roughly speaking a note on the keyboard is a finger's breadth. And you will find that an octave jump is roughly a hand's stretch. You would be wise if you discovered how much more or less than a hand's stretch it is for you personally. Try it with each hand.

The next stage in this distance-judging process might be to find a great deal of music in which the right-hand melody notes are fairly close to each other, where you do not have jumps much more than an octave which you cannot judge, and the left-hand notes are either a simple accompaniment or else melodically close to each other, as in much of Bach. If you feel that you are really insecure as a sight-reader, but would like to be better at it, then play a lot of this simple kind of music *without looking at your hands at all,* judging distances by sense of touch, not of sight. This may take a great deal of determination on your part, if you happen to be a player who has hitherto had to look down at his hands to find any note. But it is so important a part of your equipment to acquire this tactile sense of the keyboard that I strongly urge you to do it. Take a piece which you think will not be too difficult for this purpose and decide not to look at your hands at all while you are playing it. If you come to grief somewhere, find out what distance you failed to judge and find some way of judging it.

Your sense of locality on the keyboard, based on finger-breadths and hand stretches in the elementary stages, can be helped if you are aware of the patterns of the black keys in relation to those of the white ones. If, for instance, you had to play this with the fingering marked:

Example 2

you could practise judging the distances by, in the first place, feeling the black keys in between the notes; but soon you should be able to play the notes without doing so. The feeling of the black keys is only a means to learning the distances of the jumps without feeling the black keys!

At this point I should warn you of a difficulty, seldom referred to in the textbooks, affecting all pianists. There is a conflict of technical habits between the player who was taught early on to 'sight-read' and the one whose early training was mostly in technique—how to manage his hands and arms. The first player can usually play fairly well at sight, but seldom memorizes anything, the second one can play from memory fairly easily but cannot read anything easily at sight. The reason is that the first player, the better 'reader', was taught to play without looking at his hands, and the second one looked at his hands most of the time. I suppose I must have met hundreds of amateur pianists in my time, and almost all of them fell into one of these two categories. The question now is, which one should you belong to?

I can give you an answer to that one—it is 'both'! You cannot play anything much if your technique has been entirely neglected and your memory hopeless; and it is as foolish to learn the piano without learning how to read music at sight as it would be to learn English in the same way. Suppose you couldn't read a sentence in English unless you had learned it nearly by heart first!

The point is that there are two different ways of practising. One in which you are learning to find your way about the keyboard mainly by sense of touch and not by looking for each note with your eyes, and the other when you must look at your hands and at the keyboard to find out what is the best way of using your fingers, hands and arms in order to obtain the sounds you want in the easiest way. Many people have come to grief because they have practised one way and neglected the other. The right thing to do is to practise each way deliberately, knowing for what purpose you are doing it. This chapter is mostly concerned with the first way.

35

GOLDEN RULE No. 5. Always know where your hands are on the keyboard
It is easy of course when you are practising some technical problem. You are looking at your hands and discovering how to manage them so that your fingers can most easily play a particular pattern of notes. It is not so easy when you are practising by tactile sense alone. But you won't master your geographical sense of the keyboard unless you do.

3. FINGERING

The keyboard of the piano is not an ideal instrument for the fingers because fingers want to curl inwards to grasp things more than they want to tap them. I have never tried to play a harp, being far from sanguine as to my future need of it, but it always looks to me a more natural instrument to play than the piano, from a fingering point of view. The white notes of the piano, too, are horribly regular, whereas one's fingers are horribly irregular, being four or five different lengths. All sorts of compromises have to be adopted to play the scale of C. And the fingers have different strengths as well as different lengths, while the keys on the keyboard are, or should be, evenly balanced. Worst of all, we are supposed nowadays to play almost as much with the thumb as with the fingers; but the thumb is not much like a finger, from a playing point of view, and has to be played in quite a different position. No wonder the older musicians avoided using it as much as possible!

The word 'fingering' means two things: the choice of finger you make in order to play a group of notes comfortably and efficiently, and the suggestions for that choice printed or written in the music in small figures under or over a note. Makers of the keyboard have arranged it so that a key is roughly a finger's breadth from the next one, and that an octave is roughly a hand's stretch. One has to say 'roughly' because naturally everyone's hand is not the same size. But the basic position of the hand is when it is poised over the keyboard with the fingers close together, each finger covering a note. So long as you keep to this basic position you can play the next note with the next finger, the next note but one, two or three with the next finger but one, two or three:

Example 3

Most editions of music have, as you know, printed 'fingering' with the notes. You may possibly have ignored these suggestions thinking that they add yet one more difficulty to the many other difficulties of piano-playing. But it is wise to notice and consider them. Nine times out of ten they will help you, which is why they are there; but it is always open to you to substitute your own fingering, once you have considered the printed ones, because some editors have peculiar ideas about fingering, and in any case someone else's ideas may not suit your hand. The same applies to suggestions in this book—they may not suit you. But please try them out first.

You will not find any fingering in Durand's editions of Debussy's piano music, because Debussy thought that every pianist should think fingering out for himself and that only he could decide what was best for his own hands. I am sure that Debussy was right, but before a pianist can think out his own fingering he must have some idea of the general principles of fingering. These I shall try to supply in what follows.

The purpose of fingering, then, is to be able to play comfortably and musically as many notes of a group as possible, without changes of position; and, when changes of position become necessary (as of course they frequently do), to contrive each change with the least possible disturbance to the flow of the music or the comfort of the hand.

37

Technique (1) The Geography of the Keyboard

The following bars from a Mozart sonata will illustrate five points:

Example 4   Mozart K 545

In the first bar the (right) hand is in the basic position, its five fingers covering the five notes C–G. In bar 2, the thumb has to stretch downwards one note to play the first note of the bar, B. This is the smallest possible extension of the basic position, done without materially altering the position of the hand. In bar 3 the first note (and the subsequent group) is so far away from the group in the first two bars that the whole position of the hand must be changed. Mozart has considerately given you a crotchet's rest in which to lift the hand off the keyboard and put it down elsewhere. But in bar 5 one can revert to a smaller change of position, the sort done in scales, by which a thumb put under the fingers (or fingers put over the thumb) makes available a new group of notes. But in this bar there is a fifth change: the substitution of the fourth finger on the last semiquaver but two in the bar for what would normally be the third finger, if one played this scale to finish where it began. The reason for the substitution is, of course, clear: to allow the hand to descend one note lower for the next, sixth, bar. And, if you were to go further into this sonata you would find it possible to do the same substitution again in the next bar. So you have made a sequential change of notes playable by a sequential change of fingering. Convenient.

To summarize:
Basic position, five fingers over five notes (bar 1).

38

Slight extension of basic position (bar 2) (and in bar 4).
Adopt scale fingering for scalic passages (bar 5).
Adapt scale fingering to play a sequence (bars 5 and 6)
Complete change of hand-position (bar 3).

All this may seem pretty obvious to you, but I suggest that it is worth thought. It is often the obvious that one neglects.

A change of fingering implies a change of position. All changes of position are slight hazards, some big hazards. But their hazardous nature can be minimized by the player being aware of the changes. If, for instance, you have to play a long succession of single semiquavers:

Example 5   Mozart K 283

Think out at what points changes of hand-position will be necessary and mark them with a pencil. Such changes may or may not coincide with the musical phrasing.

There are two facts of every pianist's life which affect fingering and cannot be altered: the shape of the keyboard and the shape of his hand.

(a) THE KEYBOARD has two levels: that of the white notes and that of the black; and since the black notes are further from the player than the white are, it is generally (I did not say 'always') better to play the black notes with the long fingers and the white ones with the short fingers, the first and fifth. This applies when a group of notes contains a mixture of black and white:

Example 6   Beethoven

Technique (1) The Geography of the Keyboard

If all the notes of a group are black, then the thumb (which conditions the position of the hand) can obviously play on a black note.

Example 7   Chopin, Op. 10 No. 5

(b) THE HAND has one very weak finger, the fourth, which is 'weak' because it is connected structurally with both the third and fifth fingers. Even the little fifth finger, though smaller and feebler, is easier to use than the fourth. It is less dependent on its neighbour and can more easily be reinforced by the hand. So avoid using third and fourth (or the fourth and fifth) in quick succession where an alternative fingering can be used:

Example 8   Beethoven, Op. 2 No. 3

Similarly, it is obviously better to use strong fingers, where possible, for notes which need to be stressed, and to use the big gap between first and second fingers for big gaps within the same hand position.

There are several other conditions which affect fingering and may modify the normal use of it:

(i) *Rapid chromatic scales* need not always be played by the conventional scale fingering for chromatic scales, which for the following passage would involve more movement than necessary. Try:

Example 9   Beethoven, Op. 31 No. 2, last movement

40

Technique (1) The Geography of the Keyboard

(ii) *Rapid changes of finger on a repeated note* are not always necessary. The hand can do a rapid repeat of a note. In this, for instance:

Example 10 (a)   Beethoven, Op. 31 No. 2, 1st movement

you can change the finger on each repeated note, because you are playing a regular downward sequence and want to move the hand gradually lower. But here:

Example 10 (b)   Beethoven, Op. 31 No. 2, 1st movement

you can do most of the repeated notes with the same finger, while the hand stays in more or less the same position, with another finger when it doesn't.

(iii) *Legato changes of position in slow music* sometimes necessitate the substitution of one finger by another on the same note without releasing the note:

Example 11   Beethoven, Op. 28

In the above example the l.h. has a staccato accompaniment, so the pedal cannot be used.

(iv) *Legato chords* are of course often played by a discreet use of the pedal to cover up finger deficiencies or impossibilities. But where the *legato* is contrived by the fingers alone, it is usually acceptable in a series of chords for some notes to be played non-*legato*, provided that *one* note in each chord moves smoothly to the corresponding note in the next chord.

41

Technique (1) The Geography of the Keyboard

Example 12

Beethoven, Op. 53 (Waldstein)

In this example the top notes, the melody, must be very smooth. It is impossible to play all the others equally smoothly.

To play the music of the early eighteenth century or earlier, a special study of the fingering conventions of the time is advisable. Consult Rosalyn Tureck's book, *An Introduction to the Performance of Bach* (O.U.P.), for Bach's fingering. In general, musicians of this period used the thumb less often than we do, but passed fingers over fingers instead. Fingering was important because of course they had no sustaining pedal. On the other hand, the harpsichord and clavichord had little sustaining power. Here is an example of Bach's music actually fingered by his son, W. F. Bach:

Example 13

J. S. Bach

This may seem to you unnecessarily complicated, but it was in the fashion of the time and in this particular case may have been partly conditioned by the ornaments.

In Bach, who was an organist, there are many occasions when one hand helps out the other, as you will know if you have played some of 'The Forty-Eight'. Sometimes one hand takes over a note before it is released by the other hand.

All fingering is, as I have said, a matter of positioning the hand. In some contexts it is possible and advisable to, as it were, anchor the thumb to one note and let the other fingers play around it:

42

Technique (1) The Geography of the Keyboard

Example 14   Chopin, Op. 25 No. 2   Brahms, Op. 119 No. 3

When the pedal is in constant and justifiable use, as in much nineteenth-century and later music, you can take a few more liberties with the fingering. Here is an awkward bit of Brahms. I have marked what I do with the pedal and the fingering I use:

Example 15   Brahms, Violin Sonata, Op. 100

Finally, there are a few occasions when two notes can be played with one thumb. You put it down 'in the crack' between the two notes.

I realize that I have only scratched the surface of this complicated topic of fingering, but I hope I have said enough to persuade you to think about it. I would like to remind you to consider carefully any printed fingering in your music and to regard it not as an extra burden but as an offer of help. Your hands and fingers are, however, yours; and you must ultimately be the person who decides how to use them. You may find, as I have, that when you want to re-learn some half-forgotten piece of music, you will want to alter the fingering of it which you once learned.

You can get much useful experience in playing melodic music at sight from Bach, especially his easy pieces in the *Anna Magdalena Büchlein*, Mozart, Schumann's *Album for the Young* and Bartók's *Mikrokosmos* and *For Children*. In the latter two composers you will also find some simple chords. I want to say something about playing chords, because I have found that in-experienced sight-readers easily take fright when they see them.

The same principles apply to the playing of chords as to the playing of melodies. You must know where your hands are on the keyboard all the time, without the help of your eyes. It is a good thing, wherever possible, to find an 'anchor' for the hand on one particular finger, usually fifth or first or second, and to practise various chord shapes from the anchor. You have to be a bit more adventurous in fingering chords than in fingering melodies, for you cannot so easily stick to the finger-per-note basis, but an anchor will help you. For instance:

Example 16   'Wild Rider' from Schumann's *Albumn for the Young*

In the above first bar, anchor your left hand on to the bottom A; then in bars 3 and 4 on to bottom E; and subsequently back to A again. If you like to look at the whole piece and possess a copy of it, you will find that much of the music of each hand consists of 'broken' chords as well as unbroken ones. If you have the energy and time to practise broken chords on your own, the exercise will be useful to you. Try one or two keys only at a time.

When you are playing detached chords or chords which you have to leave with your hands, even if you have the pedal on between them, decide the shape of your fingers for the next chord while your hands are still in the air, and then come down plonk on it with your shaped fingers. If the chords demand *legato* playing, you will have to acquire the art, which every good organist possesses, of changing fingers quickly on a note in order to squirm to the next chord without a break in the sound. It is best to practise doing this without the pedal, other-wise you cheat and fancy you are playing smoothly when you are not. I am sure that it is worth while going through the very unsatisfying process of playing hymns, carols or chants with separate hands at first in order to get good at simple chord-playing. In this kind of music you often have to use one hand, usually the right, to help the other by taking one of its notes, when the left-hand part contains a stretch too big for your hand. In the following extract from the hymn *O God our help in ages past*, play first the right-hand part by itself and be sure that your thumb knows where that middle C is, even when playing D! Your second finger can be anchored on or over E almost all the time, but in the last chord it must play the D, because here, as well as at the first chord of the previous bar, your right thumb should play the tenor note printed in the bass clef, because the left hand has a big stretch in these places. The right hand is, therefore, playing three notes, instead of the usual two, in these chords (marked X). Here is the hymn:

Example 17

Now try the left-hand part by itself. Remember that in playing *legato* chords of two notes each, you cannot always play completely *legato* with both notes. If one of the two can go smoothly to one of the following chord, a slight detachment of the other one does not greatly matter. I have put in some fingering, but change if it does not suit you. I will merely mention that at y, two minim beats before the double bar, I find my left-hand finger is 3 on this G. So I have to change the 3 to 1 on this note to play the next chord comfortably. You may not find that this situation comes to you, but be on the look-out for changing fingers anywhere in this sort of music. You may think it a difficult process at first, but it is surprising how quickly the hand gets used to doing it. Watch the hands of any organist.

Technique (1) The Geography of the Keyboard

One of the skills one gradually acquires in this business is to invent reasonable fingering as one goes along, or at least to read the printed fingering, if any. I have marked some of the fingering in the examples in this book, but sometimes I wish that printed fingering were illegal! It prevents the pianist from thinking for himself.

These few reminders in your memory about fingering:

1. The object is to enable you to play as many consecutive notes as possible without changing the position of the hand. For instance, in a scale you have eight notes to play in an octave and only five fingers. So somewhere, you must add three fingers'-worth. To do this you play 1, 2, 3 and then start again by putting thumb under so that you have five fingers to finish the scale with.

2. Having learned the ordinary scale fingering, use it as much as possible for reading pieces. These pieces, unless very modern, are related to scales, so it is reasonable to use scale fingering.

3. There are two levels on the keyboard, the black-key level and the white-key one. When your thumb is on or over a white key, then your whole hand is on the white-key level. In this case it is usually easier and better to play such black keys as you have to play, with the fingers rather than with a thumb. You can then keep your whole hand on the white-key level. If your thumb is on a black note, as in playing the chord of F sharp major, then, of course, your whole hand is on the black-key level and there is nothing against playing more thumbs on black keys.

4. Fingering involves looking ahead and taking in a whole group of notes at a time. It is worth taking much trouble to find out what suits your particular hand.

5. Study fingering in relation to the period and conventions of the piece. In Bach's day, for instance, they used the thumb less than we do and did a good deal of passing fingers over or under fingers.

6. Always have a pencil and indiarubber handy as you practise.

7. Once having decided your fingering for a piece, stick to it.

CHAPTER 4
Technique (2)

Technique means the skilled method by which you do or make something. The word is applied particularly to the arts, usually as an antithesis to what some people call 'inspiration'. In piano-playing the word technique carries with it a cloud of associations, most of them unpleasant, like finger exercises, scales, arpeggios, and such like. Conscientious students who practise the piano regularly feel guilty if they have not devoted the first half-hour or so of each practice to these things. The less conscientious ones leave them out altogether.

Yet technique can be as fascinating for the amateur pianist as it is for the amateur carpenter, or gardener or dressmaker. Have we not all at some time or other wondered how something was done? And have we not admired the person who seems to be able to do a difficult thing with ease? The real expert is always admired. But here lies the danger: it is possible to admire the way of doing something more than the something itself, the craft more than the art, the technique more than the music. There are even famous pianists who have long since forgotten to give their public music, they give them only gymnastic displays. So technique comes to be regarded as something of value in its own right, something apart from the music, something even to be studied by itself.

I can admire expertise as much as anyone. But when I go to a piano recital I want an emotional experience quite different from the kind I get from watching a man who can balance a chair on his chin. And I am certain that when the amateur pianist studies a technical problem he does it in order to play some music, not to give a breath-taking digital display. He will never be good enough anyhow to be a technical expert, but he may easily be good enough to make some music live.

So, although in the higher reaches the technique of playing the piano involves years of hard study, I think that the amateur pianist can achieve a great deal of pleasure from a little study of how to play. A little good technique, even a little learning, is only a dangerous thing if you don't know that it is a little, or whatever Pope said.

Can we discover what are 'natural' movements of the body? I think we can. They are demonstrated every day by people who are good at physical movement: the athlete, the cricketer, the footballer or the dancer, for instance. Watch an expert in any of these activities and you find that what you admire is the apparent ease with which they move. The movement itself seems natural, unforced and smooth; there are seldom any jerks or shoves, even in the quick movements. Try and analyse any one movement—the perfect forehand drive of a tennis player say—and it seems to start with almost leisurely ease; then there is a swing reinforced with muscular power, based on a balanced body, and the ball goes over the net!

Can any of this be applied to piano-playing? Most games and other pastimes involve the use of the whole body or the big limbs, but the pianist has to do so much with his individual fingers. Yet I think that the main principles of both are the same. You need a balanced body, a natural swing coming to a climax with muscular power added to it, and a relaxed recovery at the end. So, I believe that the first principle the pianist should work for is BE COMFORTABLE. Of course, there are two kinds of physical discomfort: one is when you are doing something unfamiliar and the action feels uncomfortable merely because you are unused to it, like cutting the fingernails of your right hand with your left hand, if you are a right-handed person; and there is the other kind of discomfort when you are trying to do something which your body was not designed to do, like walking backwards. Every pianist should try to distinguish between these two kinds of discomfort, get used to the first if necessary and avoid the second.

One of the most unsatisfactory words, so often used in connection with piano technique, is 'relaxation'. To many minds, including mine, the word brings an image of people lying half-asleep in deck-chairs on a sunny afternoon. Such an attitude is far from appropriate to piano-playing. But the word really means 'loose and unrestricted', a physical state which may be the prelude to rapid or skilled movement. I wish there were an English word which conveyed the idea of ease before action, but I do not know one. I can only suggest that you think of a cat again—I can never forget that Mog—and you will see what I mean.

Sit at the piano and try hanging your arms down by your sides loosely. If you do this, you will see that your fingers are naturally curved and the palm of the hand forms a small 'cup' into which you could fit a small apple or plum. Draw one hand up and turn it over so that the palm is underneath. Now let the hand drop from the wrist, so that it hangs loose from the forearm, and lower the whole outfit on to the keyboard. Your middle three fingers will be the first to touch the keys. As they touch, the weight of the arm is for the moment supported by them. Go on letting everything go except the last joint (the one nearest the nail) of each of the three fingers, so that your hand is still connected with the keys, but the wrist has given way and the hand has sunk below the level of the fingers. Your first and fifth fingers are off the keyboard altogether. When you have gone as far as is comfortable without falling off the keyboard, start the reverse process: pull the arm up again, drawing up first the wrist, then the fingers off the keys until the hand is left hanging loosely over the keyboard as it was originally. Try both these movements several times and notice that you can alter the kind of smudgy sound your fingers make by altering the amount of arm-weight you allow to flow into them.

This is not an exercise in how to play the piano, merely one in discovering how an arm can work when it is relaxed, how weight can control tone, that your first and fifth fingers are off the keyboard and finally that the 'cup-shaped' hand is a natural one to adopt. All skilled movement is a mixture of intense energy and relaxation. In the craft of piano-playing this is particularly true for the fingers and, to a lesser extent, the hand, have to be active and energetic at times; but this energy is more effective if used to reinforce the natural movements of the limbs concerned and go with the force of gravity when time and direction permit.

I have stressed the importance of the arm first because the arm must be mobile and free if the hand and fingers are to work properly. With your left hand, grip your right forearm just below the elbow and waggle your right-hand fingers. You can easily feel the movement inside the forearm. And if you press your right-hand fingers hard on to the keys of a piano or on to a table, your left-handed grip, transferred to the upper arm, could feel the tension of the triceps. You can prove to yourself that the state of the whole arm affects the fingers; or, if you like, that tensed fingers affect the whole arm. Unfortunately, there are so many difficulties in piano-playing which tend to cause anxiety to the pianist, that he will often tense his muscles unconsciously. So it is vital to learn what it feels like to have relaxed muscles and easy, balanced movements.

In general, the quicker the music you want to play, the smaller the limb you use to play it. Rapid scalic passages can be played only by the fingers, moderately fast staccato chords by the hand, and slow romantic tunes with the whole weight of the arm flowing into the fingers. The hardest things to do in piano-playing are those in which a limb has to move faster than nature intended it to move, as in the octaves scales of the last movement of Beethoven's 'Waldstein' sonata. But remember that the arm controls everything, not always by active participation but sometimes by supporting its own weight leaving the fingers free. It also controls the position of the hands and fingers.

There are two kinds of physical movement in piano-playing.

These are preparatory and playing movements. The preparatory movements are made in order to get the fingers into the most convenient position for playing whatever comes next to be played. Many pianists become despondent because they have never realized the importance of these preparatory movements, or even that positioning is necessary at all. But I can assure you that they are just as necessary at the keyboard as they are on a tennis court or at the wicket. Players who not only sit badly, but also find their hands and fingers always trying to do awkward contortions, are usually ignorant of preparatory movements. We shall see, when we come on to details, how much the arm plays an important part in them.

Then there are playing movements. These are comparatively simple, once a good position has been achieved, being normally straight down, though in some situations the finger appears to make an oblique and downward movement. The critical thing here is not so much the direction of the movement as its speed and extent. The intensity of the tone of a note, its loudness or softness, depends mostly on the speed with which you put down a key. It also depends on how far the key is depressed. When you depress a key you are throwing a small hammer against the string to make a sound. You can do this by a quick but short-distanced tap on the key. Put a small book or a matchbox just under the lip of the white keys, so that they cannot be depressed fully, and tap them hard. The notes will sound, but with a thin tone. This is the sort of action you set in motion when you play quick scales or scalic passages. You cannot play quick scales very loudly, because there is not time for the keys to get to the bottom.

Part of the playing movement is to stop playing! Or, if you like, you can think of the stopping as part of the preparation movement for the next note. In any case, the release of a key is important. I think the easiest way of thinking of this release is to have in your mind a basic position for the hands, just above the keys, to which you revert after every playing movement, unless, of course, you are playing a *legato* passage which involves going on to the next note at the actual moment of releasing the one before. Even then, the releasing finger resumes its normal position.

I very much dislike describing these technicalities in a way to suggest that the hand does this or the fingers do that or the arm does something else. All interact with each other most of the time. But it is true that the fingers must sometimes act as independently as possible from the arm and hand, though not as often as some people think, I believe. The weak fifth finger, for instance, can hardly play anything without a little help from the hand; and even the most adventurous finger makes best use of its independence if it can feel that the hand to which it belongs and the arm behind the hand are in support of it. That support may not itself be active, but it is there. The solitary policeman who finds it necessary to take individual action does so with more confidence and efficiency because he knows that the whole police force and the Law behind the police will support him. The finger does not think like the policeman, but it can feel, and it will work best if the hand and arm are so positioned behind it as to make its work easy. The player who stretches a finger out in one direction while his arm is pulling in another finds piano-playing more difficult than it need be.

There are, therefore, three separate actions involved in the playing of every note or chord: first, getting into the best possible position for playing it; second, playing it, and third, releasing it so as to be ready to adopt a new position for what follows. The fluent pianist of course merges these three actions into one, but if you are not fluent in any particular situation it is as well to break down your actions into these thoughtful three sections. And remember that a mistake or a difficulty in playing one particular note may be due to the way you left the one before. In particular, the very start of a piece or the start of a new phrase may so easily be badly done because the hand is not in a good position to play it. It is certain that many pianists make bad starts because they are too scared to leave the keyboard. They hang on to it as if it were the last thing between them and drowning. So they never get used to a good clean start, even at the very beginning of a piece of music.

Big jumps are difficult for some people, partly because they do not always know exactly where they are going (memorizing is most helpful here) and partly because they lose balance while the hand is jumping. I am thinking of the sort of thing you get in Chopin waltzes—or any other waltz, for that matter, where there are jumps in the left hand of more than an octave—in which the left hand has to play a note low in the bass clef followed by a chord about the middle of the piano, like this:

Example 18   Chopin, Op. 64 No. 2

The secret is to release the bottom note quickly, move very quickly to a position directly over the chord, and then move down to play. In early practice you may have to stop the movement of the hand over the chord until you are sure that you are in the right position, and then move down to play. Later the movement is all one, nearly. The bigger the jump the faster the hand has to move in the air. Sometimes, of course, the hand has to go down again to a bottom note as fast as it went up, as in this Brahms waltz, in which both hands have big jumps.

Example 19   Brahms, Op. 39

When the remote bottom note is a single one and not, as in the Brahms example, an octave, it is not necessary to play it with the forearm straight behind the finger, as you would were the note in the middle of the piano. In the Chopin waltz, think of the left hand being balanced mainly over the *chords* in the middle of the piano and the little finger darting downwards to the C sharp, or whatever it is, and playing it at an angle. You would have to do this to play the very bottom note of the piano, because it is too far to play 'straight' without getting off the piano stool and walking down to the bass end of the instrument!

This playing of extreme notes at an angle to the line of the keyboard applies also to less extreme ones which have to be played quickly. Often a quick turn of the hand can solve the difficulty. For instance:

Example 20   Chopin, Waltz, Op. 42

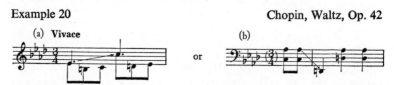

Besides turning laterally as in Example 20, the hand itself can actually play the piano, you will be surprised to hear. But in most cases of rapid or fairly rapid music, consisting usually of small chords, the hand does best if it is, as it were, shaken out of the arm and left to do its own bouncing as a result of the shaking. In a passage like this, for instance:

Example 21

I should play the first chord with the arm coming down fairly vigorously on the keys and coming up again on the last chord of each bar. The chords in between I should play with small hand bounces which have been sparked off by the arm at the start. Something of the same technique might come in handy in the famous and difficult start to a movement of a Beethoven sonata:

Example 22   Beethoven, Op. 2 No. 3

(a) **Allegro assai**

One difficulty here is changing direction at the beginning; another is to play so many chords at a stretch and rapidly. In order to get gradually accustomed to these difficulties, practise the passage beginning at the second chord, leaving out the first one, and in brief bits, perhaps four chords at a time, like this:

(b)

The same kind of practising can be given to octaves, which are harder to play than sixths. Start by doing very small stretches and then gradually play longer ones:

(c)

Later difficulties involve the adjustments necessary to play a mixture of white and black notes; and a change of direction from down to up or vice versa:

Brahms, Op. 39

(d)   **Tempo giusto**

Experiment for yourself and see what happens, or imagine what could happen when you are used to it. Of course, you can use the hand as a hand for single notes as well as for chords.

But I should be chary of ever saying that I use only the hand for anything. The arm always has a hand in it, and this is not meant to be funny!

THE PEDAL

I am talking here, of course, of the sustaining pedal, not the 'soft' one. The misuse of the pedal does more to spoil the playing of a moderate performer than anything else, except a multitude of wrong notes. But it is not at all difficult to learn how to use it properly.

The first thing is **GOLDEN RULE No. 6. Pedal with your ears!** The exclamation mark is intended to imply that the intention of this advice is metaphorical, not literal. I do not want you to press down the pedal with your head. I want you to determine when and when not to pedal by listening to the result of each process. But I also suggest that you deliberately play to yourself several yards of Bach three times a week, using music that needs to be played *legato* and music that needs to be played *staccato*, without using the pedal at all. Your ears must get used to the wonderfully clean sound of un-pedalled music, if by any chance they have become sullied by the habit of over-pedalling for years. It will also do your technique no harm to play *legato* with your fingers and *staccato* with your fingers and your ears.

I am sure that someone once taught you how to use the sustaining pedal, so you know how to, even if you don't do it. One of the points of having a pedal at all is, of course, to keep notes sounding when your hand can't keep the keys down.

Composers of the nineteenth and twentieth centuries have been occasionally careless about indications for pedalling, sometimes putting *staccato* marks and pedal marks for the same notes. One just has to use one's own judgement, which means that one must decide, by really hard, attentive listening, whether notes or chords that should not smudge together are, in fact, being smudged, and whether rests marked in the music really mean silences or not. In romantic music the pedal can sometimes be rightly used to create a general resonance rather than for the purpose of connecting two or more particular notes or chords, and the same can apply to early twentieth-century music of the impressionist type. Beethoven, whose pedal was probably not as powerful in effect as in a modern grand piano, did what might almost be called 'impressionistic' things with the pedal— in the D minor Sonata, Op. 31 No. 2, for instance—and of course Debussy is full of places where a misty, slightly confused sound is obviously what he wanted. But generally speaking, one should change the pedal when a complete change of harmony occurs, and in dances like waltzes, gavottes, etc., where a short silence, often at the end of a bar, gives a lift to the rhythm, it is better to use too little pedal than too much. If in doubt, play a line or two without any pedal at all just to find out for yourself how much the pedal is really needed.

One of the less pleasant habits which some pianists acquire by habit rather than intentionally is playing the left hand slightly ahead of the right in places where both hands should be dead together. Sometimes this is caused by either (i) a hardly conscious desire to obtain extra emphasis with the right hand, or (ii) the simple physical fact that the left hand starts a bit closer to the keyboard than the right hand and consequently gets there first. The cure is, of course, to listen while playing some piece full of staccato chords for both hands (Beethoven Sonata, Op. 14 No. 2 in G, second movement would do) and making sure that the hands are together in sound. The desire for extra emphasis, so often displayed by the poor organist who puts his foot down on a pedal note just before his hands each time, is irritating and ineffective, both for the same reason—it happens too often. A very occasional chord spread so as to give an unusual accent to the top note may be justified. The Kreutzer sonata for violin and piano starts with one. I suppose that if you wanted to give a particular word, say the word 'terrific' an added punch you might pronounce it with a delayed first syllable and say 'turr-ific'. But to do it often would be like having toffee for every meal, and as someone in *Iolanthe* said: nauseating.

Technique should, of course, always be geared towards a musical purpose, but there are occasions when the learning of a difficult passage is difficult because the musical phrasing obscures the mechanical pattern. Suppose, for instance, that your left hand had to play this:

Example 23   Brahms, Op. 38

It looks annoyingly hard. But practise it like this:

and it becomes easy, because your mind has suddenly seen the plan. Chopin has this in his Study in G flat, Op. 10 No. 5 (Example (a)). But try it as in (b) and it is much easier:

Example 24

A whole book could be, and perhaps has been, written on the psychology of piano practice. I can only give you a very few ideas here. But do not forget that there are two aspects of every technical problem: the *mental* and the *physical*, and the mental one should be tackled first. If you have a cloud of twelve or sixteen semiquavers on paper, looking like a plague of locusts, organize them into groups so that your mind can get hold of them. Do not hesitate to alter temporarily the rhythm of an

Technique (2)

awkward passage if by doing so you can make it clearer to your mind and therefore easier for your fingers. Seek out, in any passage of many notes, particular notes as landmarks for your fingers to aim at, whether they are musically important or not; and do not scruple to alter a marked fingering to suit yourself, and to help your hands to combine with each other. Your body has a natural symmetry not only of shape but of movement. It is easier to play the first and second fingers of one hand with the first and second fingers of the other than with the second and first of the other.

Example 25   Beethoven, Op. 69

The details of how technique can be applied to particular situations will, I hope, become clear in the following chapters which deal with specific pieces of music. I should like now to summarize what seem to me to be the most important of the general principles which I have outlined in this and the previous chapter.

1. All skilled movement is a mixture of muscular energy alternated with the kind of relaxation which prepares for that energy. Since effective movement in one direction is nearly always the natural reaction from movement in the opposite direction, a balanced body, arms and hands are an essential preliminary to good piano-playing.

2. Purposeful movement is, in the early stages at least, the result of purposeful thought. It is, therefore, necessary for a player to know exactly what he wants to do with his fingers before he does it. At a later stage, after the careful and constant practice of skilled movements, the thoughts become so automatic as to be hardly conscious. But all the time it is the

59

Technique (2)

thoughts and not only the movements which should be automatic. The mind should always hold a general watching brief
over the fingers.

3. There are two kinds of physical movements in piano-playing:
the preparatory and the playing movements. It is as vital to
be in the right position to play every note that you want to
play on the piano as it is to be in the right position to return
a service at tennis or play a ball from the bowler at cricket.

4. The fingers are in action all the time. In rapid passages they
work without forceful help from the hand or arm. Particular
care is needed to play thumbs independently of the larger
limbs. But the arm and hand should be always in support
of the fingers in creating positional comfort and, in slower
or more expressive music, in taking an active and supporting
part in playing.

5. Pedal with the ears.

CHAPTER 5

Technique (3): Arpeggios and Scales

Most amateur pianists think of arpeggios and scales with distaste. They feel that they ought to practise them, but never want
to do so because they seem to be purely technical exercises with
no music in them. I sympathize with this attitude and remember
with clarity and horror the struggle I had with the wretched
things when I was compelled to enter an Associated Board
examination at the age of about fourteen. But I did them and,
although I have not always thought affectionately of the Associated Board since then, I am intensely grateful to it for making
me learn my scales and arpeggios.

I am grateful for two reasons: physical and mental. Most of
the piano music that you and I play is based on the conventional diatonic system of the last three hundred years. Once
my fingers had got used to scales and arpeggios, I found I could
cope physically with a good many of the scalic and chordal
passages I was required to play, though of course there was
much music that was too difficult for me. And since scales and
arpeggios are a sort of summary of the conventions of musical
texture, I found that the whole complex key system was not so
complex after all. I could understand it without much further
effort. And of course when I came to learn 'intervals' and
elementary harmony, I understood what they were all based on.
I am now sure that it would be as unwise to avoid learning
scales and arpeggios if one wants to play an instrument or be
any good as a musician, as it would be to avoid learning how
to count up to ten if one wants to be a mathematician, or
avoid recognition of letters if one wants to learn how to read
English. Bertrand Russell once said that nobody is born with

an innate desire to learn the multiplication table, but it has to be learned!

Of course, one's taste or distaste for scales and arpeggios depends on how one learns them. There are some people who hate thinking so much that they positively enjoy some purely mechanical action. Quite young children are often stunningly competent at scales, and rattle them off with the slightest encouragement. But, although digital dexterity is certainly one of the objects of learning scales, I am sure that understanding both of their make-up and of how to play them, should come first.

The make-up of diatonic scales, major or minor, is quite easy to learn. It is simply a matter of the position of the semitones, which is relatively the same in all major keys. The two minor scales have different arrangements of semitones, but once you have learned them you find that they are the same in all keys. If you are not sure what these arrangements are, notice where, that is on which degrees of the scale, the semitones come in some scale you know, and then apply this knowledge to all other scales of the same kind. The only thing you must remember, if you want to write one down or name its notes, is that the same alphabetical letter comes only once within each octave. You never have, say, an F and an F sharp in the same scale: if you have an F sharp, the first note below it must be E sharp, if it looks like F on the keyboard. You should call it E sharp and write it as E sharp, as in the key of F sharp major. So all scales have a straight series of seven alphabetical letters in them, though some of them may have the word 'flat', 'sharp' or even 'double-sharp' added to the alphabetical letter. This may seem unnecessarily confusing to you, but if you think for a moment you will see that scales could not logically be written otherwise. You could not very well have a key signature in which a note was both flat and sharp!

But let us get on to the playing. I should like to discuss the playing of arpeggios before that of scales, because an arpeggio has fewer notes than a scale but has wider intervals between the

notes, so that the chief difficulty—which is putting the thumb
under the fingers—is encountered in its most acute form. This
difficulty occurs, of course, in the playing of scales too, but
there is something to be said for tackling it at its widest and
worst.

But before we worry about putting thumbs under fingers,
we may as well just glance at a single-octave arpeggio, in which
you do not have to put the thumb under at all. Try the right
hand in D major for instance:

Example 26

There is nothing very difficult about this, because the short
thumb and fifth finger have white notes to play and the only
black note is played with the longer second finger. Arpeggios
of E major, A major and B major are similarly convenient,
especially that of B major, where both the long fingers have the
black middle notes.

Don't forget to do the left hand: at first play the mirror image
of the right.

In all these easy arpeggios (and in all others, too) it is important to allow the arm to shift a very little, as you play, from
the thumb towards the fifth finger (and, of course, back again),
so that each finger knows it has the arm behind it. These movements are still *very small* and you might almost think of them
as not movements at all, but just as an easing of the hand in

the direction in which the fingers are leading you. But this 'easing' makes all the difference between comfort and discomfort, ease and difficulty, and in the end between being able to play fast easily and not being able to play fast.

I now suggest that you play each of these arpeggios—if you feel happy about what you have done already—with one more note at the end and by putting the thumb on the fourth note. This is very tricky and very important. If you learn to do this well, all scales and arpeggios will be easier for you. Try first with B major. Put your right-hand fingers over the first three notes, then play them, but pause with your third finger on the F sharp. Then pivot your hand on the F sharp (without letting it go) so that your thumb travels under your fingers to the B. You may raise your wrist a little to allow room for the thumb to go under. As you play the thumb on B, you let go the third finger on its F sharp and immediately straighten the hand, pivoting on the B, so that all your fingers cover the next three or four notes of the arpeggio. Then play only one more note, the D sharp with your second finger. Do all this very slowly at first, but the straightening of the hand quicker than all the other movements.

Example 27

Then do the same actions with the left hand, downwards.

This is, as you will see, the famous 'thumb under' difficulty. It needs to be thought about, practised and *felt*. Do all this very slowly at first until you find it comfortable to do, and if you do not agree with the suggestions I have already made—

try some other way of your own. When you are fairly used to doing it with each hand, then try it a little faster, and then in different rhythms and with differing musical purposes. Here are some possibilities:

Example 28

Of course when you can go in one direction easily, try going both ways, there and back. Then try in other keys of roughly the same arpeggio shape, then in keys which are all white notes, such as C major or E minor, which I always think are harder to play than B major, because you have to make your longer fingers play notes which are nearer to you than black ones would be. So for the middle white notes you have to curl your middle fingers, second and third, a little more than you did when they were playing black notes. Finally, try some of those arpeggios which start with a black note. They are usually played in the right hand with the second finger playing the first note and the thumb going under for the first white note, as in E flat or A flat or B flat major. The left hand follows the same principle. Here are two of them, one for each hand:

Example 29

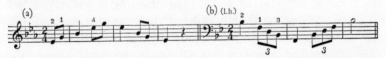

So far I have suggested the fingering usually taught in England. But for some arpeggios (not all) a different fingering may be preferable. This means playing the largest gap between two consecutive notes with the two fingers which have the largest span between them, such as:

E   65

Example 30

There is one disadvantage in this fingering. Find out what it is. Then decide whether for you the disadvantage outweighs the obvious advantage of playing a big note-gap with a big finger-gap. Incidentally, do not be the slave of anyone else's conventional fingering, find out your own. I'm not saying that the conventional fingering is necessarily bad, usually it is the best. But on principle, question it at first and substitute another if you want to. How would you finger, for instance, the horrible arpeggio of F sharp major?

I hope you are keen enough to want to explore, or become more familiar with, other arpeggios besides those of the ordinary major and minor common chords: the dominant and diminished seventh ones, for instance. These occur so frequently in classical music that it is well worth while to know them intimately; and if you want to know any chord well, it is not enough merely to know it theoretically from a book on harmony—you must do something active about it. Play its arpeggio. Diminished sevenths are fairly easy to learn and to play, partly because there are only three of them and partly because they all contain a series of the same interval—minor thirds. Fingering is easy if you go on the principle of keeping your thumb for white notes. But dominant sevenths are rather harder. The important thing to discover for yourself about their fingering is where you feel it easiest to put the thumb under. Experiment for yourself and do not necessarily do the same fingering for different keys. The diminished sevenths are all much the same shape: the dominant sevenths are all different shapes. Here for instance:

Example 31

Technique (3) Arpeggios and Scales

In general I suggest that you do not try to practise dozens of arpeggios at the same practice, unless they are all familiar to you. It is better to find out which ones are used frequently in any piece of music you happen to want to learn, even if there are only two or three of them, and then practise all varieties of them rather than range indefinitely over many different ones. Specific objectives are always better than general objectives, because you can see the results of your efforts more quickly. If I were learning Beethoven's first piano sonata (in F minor) I would make a dead set at the arpeggios of F minor and A flat major to start with, not to mention a few mixtures of dominant and diminished seventh ones.

SCALES

I have already said something about the make-up of scales, so let us now think of the playing of them. To be able to play them fluently is, of course, immensely valuable to you as a pianist, partly because so much music contains scale fragments, is based on keys of which the scale is a summary and involves the quick playing of notes near to each other, which of course is just the very thing that scale technique enables you to do.

You have to put the thumb under fingers even in a single octave of a scale, because you only have five fingers and there are eight notes in a scale of one octave. If you have learned how to do this in arpeggios, you will find it easier to do in scales, especially if you maintain your hand at an angle to the keys, giving the thumb less far to go. I find it easier to do this thumb-under process just after the finger has played a black note, as in the scale of D in the right hand or a downward scale of E in the left, but in the end you have to do it after a finger on a white note, as in the scale of C major, so you may as well face it. Do all this experimental practising very slowly at first, and do not scruple to look at your hands to see what they are up to. When you are completely used to the 'feel' of them, then you can play them without looking at your fingers.

Technique (3) Arpeggios and Scales

One thing I should have mentioned when dealing with arpeggios, and it certainly applies to scales is that the moment your thumb has left the last note it played, it should begin to move under the fingers in preparation for its next note; and the hand movement also is a gradual one which begins a little time before it is absolutely necessary. In other words, neither the movement of the thumb nor that of the hand is a sudden movement. Imagine that both your thumb and your hand have a mind of their own and know what they are going to have to do in two or three notes' time. The only thing that *is* sudden and quick is the straightening of the hand after the thumb has played.

It is worth while, I think, practising this thumb-under business with very small groups of notes, groups of five or six notes in a strong rhythm, preferably in an easy key like D for the right hand (or a downward C minor melodic in the left). I always think that C major is one of the nastiest of all scales to play: it has no landmarks, no easy black-note drops to white-note thumbs, and it sounds dull somehow, anyhow. Here are your five or six notes in a reasonable key:

Example 32

Scales are often thought of as boring exercises because people tend to play them in the same way all the time, straight through from top to bottom and back without any variation of rhythm. In fact, one very seldom finds in a piece of music a scale of that kind with both hands together; and I am sure that there is a lot to be said for practising scales (a) with hands separately, (b) in different rhythmic patterns of your own invention, and (c) in fragments, according to what you find needs most practice, and with some musical purpose. Here are a few examples of such fragments: notice the metronome pace-marks. You can and should invent many other fragments of your own.

Technique (3) Arpeggios and Scales

Example 33

Finally, may I remind you that you can do all your scale or arpeggio practising without a book, that is without the distraction of having to read music. You can give your whole attention to your hands and fingers. And when you find yourself improving at them, you will be glad to have developed some digital dexterity and a sense of key, things which will last you all your life.

At this point we must pay some thought to the fingers themselves, for after all it is the fingers that do all playing, even if they are helped by the hand and arm to some extent. How does one really use the fingers?

In ordinary life one uses the fingers rather differently from the way in which piano-playing demands. To pick things up or twist things one uses the fingers—the four fingers as opposed to the thumb, I mean—more or less together. All four fingers move in the same direction and the thumb is used in opposition to them. But in piano-playing one has to use the fingers independently of each other, and the thumb is used almost as another finger, but turned on its side and hitting notes with its side. This independence of the fingers cannot be completely achieved, because the fourth finger in each hand has a tendon inside the hand which connects it to both the fifth and the third fingers. That is why it is so difficult to play a trill with third and fourth fingers and even more difficult to do so with fourth and fifth fingers, both weak ones. So, in general, it is better to play quick trills with alternate rather than adjacent fingers, though if one of the fingers is the second it is not hard to use the third for the other one.

Technique (3) Arpeggios and Scales

When I started learning the piano at the age of about eight, I was made to hold down all the fingers but one and play with the one. This was agony if the playing one was the fourth, but I was told that the exercise was wonderful for 'strengthening the fingers'. Of course, we all know that a muscle that is constantly used tends to become stronger, or at any rate can do more easily what you want it to do. But I am quite sure that this holding down of all the fingers but one, was not a good idea. In fact, I do not think that the amateur pianist should do it at all, and I'm not at all sure that 'strengthening the fingers' is what one ought to aim at. I do not know enough about anatomy to tell you exactly what happens to muscles and tendons when you exercise them very hard, but I am certain that one should never try to force fingers—or any other limbs—to make movements which they really cannot do. What one can do is to use possible movements often, carefully and slowly at first until the tendons and muscles get accustomed to unfamiliar actions. By degrees what was at first strange and awkward becomes possible and then actually easy.

On the other hand, do not jump to the conclusion that the fingers can be lazy. Nothing is further from the truth. Your fingers must learn to be energetic, each one individually. The hand must help the fingers of course, that is, it must be in the right position to make finger-movement easy or it may even reinforce the finger movement, especially in the case of the fourth and fifth fingers; but it should never take the place of finger energy. (You can discover how easy it is to forget to use energetic fingers when you play big chords. Try Chopin's easy and famous 20th Prelude in C minor, and you will find yourself neglecting the inside fingers of the right-hand chords. Even soft chords need individual finger energy.)

Fingers need energy not only in a downward direction to play notes, but also in an upward direction to release them. This does not mean (as I was once taught) that you have to pull each finger up from a note so far that it curls up almost above the level of the back of your hand, but simply that you must be

70

Technique (3) Arpeggios and Scales

able to bounce the fingers off notes. The spring under the key helps the finger up again, it is only a very small movement, but it must be done in *staccato* passages or where the finger has to move quickly elsewhere to play another note. In other words, fingers should at all times be *alive* and buoyant. Try sometimes a short exercise with your hand balanced on its thumb and the fingers playing *staccato*:

Example 34

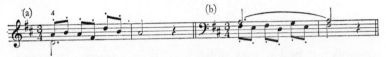

It is not always easy to say how much the hand helps the fingers to play. I hope that my own fingers are fairly active, but sometimes I have a suspicion that my hand always helps them. Roughly speaking, the slower and louder one plays, the more one's hand comes into action, and behind the hand, the arm. In this for instance:

Example 35   Beethoven, Op. 10 No. 3

I suggest that if you haven't done much of this, a good deal of experiment with slow sentimental tunes would be a useful experience for you. Chopin's Nocturnes are full of them; or, if you hate them, try some Beethoven slow movements.

But what you probably want to know is how to play fast. I can give you no elixir that will enable you to play the Minute Waltz in a minute tomorrow if you can't today, because playing fast is, as I have already implied, a matter of getting used to new and small actions; and this takes time. Most fast playing is done by the fingers, with only very little playing help from the hands or arms. The hands and arms are too big and clumsy to play lots of notes very fast, though, of course, you have to be sure that they are in a position to allow your fingers to move fast, when they must. If, for instance, you want to play:

Example 36

you will not find it very difficult: it is an ordinary arpeggio. What you are doing is transferring the weight of your arm from the little finger on the first note to the thumb on the last one. But try now to play this extract from Beethoven's Sonata, Op. 2 No. 2 in A:

Example 37

and you will find it harder, even though the first five notes are the same as in the previous example, though in a different order. Why is it harder? Because you need quite a different technique from that used before. You need what is called forearm rotation.

The great piano-teacher Tobias Matthay was, I think, the first to call attention to the 'element', as he called it, of forearm rotation which all the great pianists have used, consciously or not, and which is a necessity in all piano-playing. Matthay called it an 'element' because it is not necessarily a movement and cannot always be seen. No doubt you have heard of it, though you may not be aware that to play the piano fluently you use it all the time.

Forearm rotation is the exertion you use in your forearm to

screw or unscrew a screw, to wind up a watch or to turn a door-handle. If you put your left-hand third finger on G sharp and hold it down, then play the E below with your fifth finger and 'woggle' on to the top E with your thumb, you are using this rotation. There are many occasions when you use the same kind of energy, or release of energy, without actually moving anything visibly. The point is that merely to exert a very small amount of energy of the forearm in the direction of the finger you are just about to play and at the same time stop using it in the opposite direction, you are helping the fingers to play. This energy is not a substitute for finger exertion, but a necessary preliminary to it. Many would-be pianists have failed to use their fingers properly because they have, as it were, locked up their muscles with their forearms, or have tried to use two opposing muscles at the same time.

All new actions and all unfamiliar patterns must be practised slowly at first, because the communicating system between your brain and your fingers must be given a chance to become accustomed to a novelty. Get faster by degrees, as you feel it possible, but remember that speed does not mean more muscular effort. The faster you go, the lighter your hand may have to be; and, in a sense, the lighter-hearted your mind.

CHAPTER 6

Memorizing

I believe that all pianists, however young or old, good or bad, should learn how to play from memory. But before you hold up your hands in horror and say that you have never been able to memorize things and don't see why you should, since you have no ambition to become a concert pianist, hold on a moment till I tell you why I believe in memorizing.

First, I think it is the natural thing to do. If you have a good tune in your head, your natural impulse is to sing it, or whistle it or hum it. If your 'tune' is more than just a melody, but a whole piece for the piano, you would still want to do the same thing. If you knew you could, you would want to go to the piano and play it—without bothering to search for the music. That is what fiddlers used to do when they played folk tunes and country dances in pubs; and that is what jazz players and pop singers still do when they want to entertain either themselves or us. That is what every really good musician would do who had music in his head and wanted to play it to someone.

Secondly, I am quite sure that if you have music in your head and have taught your fingers to play it 'out of your head', so to speak, all sorts of things become technically easier, and you can play more happily. If you know what sound you want and know that, say, F sharp is the note that will give you that sound, then you play F sharp on purpose. You don't play it merely automatically because your finger has played it a hundred times before; and you don't play it automatically because a blob on the music says play it.

I had better say that I am advocating memory-playing *not* because I am thinking of you as a concert pianist who can play

a concerto for three-quarters of an hour without music. I am
not concerned here with such feats. I am not wanting you to
do prodigious feats of memory, nor even to play all the time
without music in front of you. What I am concerned with is
that you should learn as much from memory as you can by
sound and translate those sounds into finger actions. Music,
after all, deals with sounds.

Playing from memory will bring a few other accomplish-
ments in its train. You will find this out when you do it. Some
musicians—I am one, I fear—are not at all systematic; but
purposeful memorizing impels one to be orderly and to look
for orderliness in the music.

Let us think what factors go to make up a musical memory:

1. *Muscular memory*—this I have already referred to. It is certain that your fingers—or any other parts of your body for that
matter—will develop a memory of their own. This memory
works largely without your conscious control. If any of your
limbs have performed the same action often, like putting on
your shoes, walking upstairs in your home, brushing your hair
or turning the handle of a door, they can do it without any
effort on your part. Everyone who plays an instrument uses
this kind of memory; it saves a lot of trouble.

2. *'Photographic' memory*—this is a memory of the visual
image of the music. Some people have this so strongly developed
that they can remember the details of a full score, just by imagin-
ing the look of it. Most ordinary people have this gift not so
highly developed, but they can often remember the general
look of a page of music and whereabouts on it any particular
passage occurs.

3. *Analytical memory*—again, this is a memory which some
people develop to a high degree. But most people have a little
of it. Many years ago I was a candidate for entry to the Royal
College of Music, and the examiner of the aural tests gave us a

downward scale of D in a certain rhythm. Of course, we all knew it was a scale. We had, as it were, organized what we had heard and we recognized the system of the notes. I can remember it still, just as if you were to say to me 'two-four-six-eight-ten'. I should recognize the system and remember it for a long time. Clearly, the more you can make a system of the music you play, the easier it is to remember.

4. *Aural memory*—this is just a memory of the sound. Most people have a pretty good aural memory in general. Indeed, some quite untrained musicians often seem to have a better aural memory than trained ones. But here again most of us remember the general sound of the music, usually the 'tune' if there is one, and are not so good at the harmony or complex counterpoint.

The next question is, how should one use all these different kinds of memory to help one to play the piano? Perhaps there is no single answer to this, or perhaps there is a different answer for each individual player. But I am certain what is best for me and nearly certain what is worst for everyone! For me, the most important of all these memories is the aural one, to learn the actual sounds in one's head. That is the king-pin of the whole business. All the other 'memories' hang on it. But one must ideally remember not only the melody on top, but those at the bottom or in the middle, as in a Bach fugue; or in a piece of later date the tune, the bass and the harmony in between. In fact, one should remember the sound of everything in the piece.

To memorize a piece of music it is first necessary to *hear* every sound in the piece; and it is surprising how much one does not hear till one tries. Then the next stage is to discover what notes make the sounds one has heard. Of course, the piece will tell you this; but I suggest that you should know it yourself, without having to 'finger' the piece to get your fingers to tell you. I must admit to you that I have often reverted to bad habits of my youth and sometimes tried to rely on my fingers only to memorize something. Sometimes that works for a time, but sooner or later it lets me down and I am stuck, quite unable to go on. But if I make myself remember the *sounds* I need, then I know I can get on again and get on securely.

If you go to a doctor with an obscure complaint he will make more than one test before making a diagnosis. It is safer to cross-check symptoms. The same applies in memorizing music. If you have remembered some music by sound in your head and have a general idea of what notes make the sounds, use all the other 'memories' I have mentioned to cross-check your aural memory. This is, of course, where your muscular memory comes in. Your fingers will easily confirm what your ear tells you is right. But do not rely only on that: analyse the music into some sort of 'system' as much as you can, whether it be harmonic progressions (if you know some harmony) or sequences, inversions, key-changes, or just a plain line of notes going steadily up or down. All these things, so dull to read about in a text book of old-fashioned harmony or 'form', can come alive in a piece the moment you see that you can use them.

I suggest now that you take an easy piece such as the first of Schumann's *Kinderscenen*, called *Von fremden Ländern und Menschen* ('Of strange countries and peoples'), Op. 15, and play it over several times until you know something of it. It has, as you see, a simple tune on top, a detached bass underneath and a triplet accompaniment in the middle—all this in the first half of the piece. Learn first the tune by sound, until you could sing it without any music. Then learn the bass quavers as if they made a tune, which they almost do. You can also discover that the first half of the piece is eight bars long, that the first two phrases, each two bars long, are identical; and the third phrase starts the same as the first one but has an 'end' tacked on to it of two more bars. So your first half is, in bars, 2 + 2 + 4. Incidentally, the last eight bars of the piece are almost the same as the first eight. After the double-bar there is a middle section of 2 + 2 + 2 bars. In both the middle section and the main sections of the piece the two hands move roughly in contrary motion.

See if you can play (a) the right hand separately, and (b) the left-hand 'tune' separately from memory. (Use the fingering you would have to use for the complete piece.) Then both together, but without the triplets in the middle, like this:

Example 38

The inside triplets are the hardest part of the piece to remember, but not really difficult if you know a little elementary harmony. It might be a good thing to play them as chords, taking two notes with the left hand and one with the right in the first half of the piece, and to discover what chords they are. They are all quite ordinary chords, but the last beat of bars 1 and 3 are diminished sevenths; and in bar 7 the left hand G is a hangover from the G in the bar before and therefore a suspension which falls to its natural resolution, F sharp, on the next beat. Almost all pieces get a little more complicated after the first exposition of the main themes, and this little piece is no exception. The six bars after the double bar are a bit more complex: the lay-out is slightly different to start with, the right hand having two notes at once in each chord and the left hand only one; and the chords at the end of the third and sixth bars after the double-bar need a little thought. Do not worry if you do not always know the right names for chords. In many cases it does not greatly matter if you think of them by the wrong grammatical name. The main point is that you should fit them into some system which you know. For instance in the third bar after the double bar, second beat, some people would call this chord an 'added sixth' (the chord of A minor plus an F sharp), but it would be just as sensible to call the C and E in the middle of the chord an appogiatura or delayed action form of B and D sharp, making the whole chord into another dim. seventh. The B and D sharp actually arrive in the next bar.

All this takes a long time to write and to check with what you find in the music, but once you have really understood it you could remember it for life! Besides, if your brain has got a hold of the 'grammar', the muscular memory of your fingers will be reinforced by your intellect, and the two memories together will make you very secure; and security will make you confident and happy.

You will, I hope, have gathered that relating sounds with written notes is most relevant to this business of memorizing music. If you know what notes make what sounds you can memorize anything—provided that you can remember the sounds. Toscanini, the great Italian conductor could, it was said, write out the full score of some large and complex piece like the Wagner Prelude to *Tristan* from memory, putting in not only the right notes but also the bowing marks and expression marks of each part. But few of us can do that, and it would be very depressing to decide that because we are not as talented as he was we are no good at all, and that trying to memorize anything is waste of time. I am sure it isn't. I am equally sure that even if one remembers only half, or even a quarter, of the whole of a piece, or if one grasps the main outline without being sure of all the details, it is worth doing. I have tried it on myself.

In the next chapter we will discuss a longer and more famous piece, from the point of view of memorizing. Meanwhile just consider that there are three parts of yourself which can remember music: your ear, your brain and your fingers. If you can combine all three, you can memorize.

CHAPTER 7

Bach's Prelude in B Minor— the Last of the Forty-Eight

A MEMORY EXERCISE

This last Prelude of all the Forty-Eight Preludes and Fugues is an easy one to play. There are very few technical difficulties, so it is a good one to learn from memory: one can give one's whole attention to memorizing it. It is also a very lovely piece of music which, for me at any rate, breathes an atmosphere of deep contentment. There is a quiet certainty about it, as in much of Bach's reflective music, which makes you feel that Bach had no doubts or worries when he wrote it. He had just found part of truth.

I do not think one can play this piece as it should be played unless one knows it, not only in one's memory but also in one's bones, so as to play it with that same quiet certainty which the music wants to convey to the listener. I do not mean that you should always play it without music, but I do mean that you should learn it from memory; and then, if you want to play it on some subsequent occasion when you may have forgotten a few details, don't scruple to have the music in front of you. But use the music only as a reminder of details, not as a general prop.

This is one of those pieces which, if you learn it by heart properly, leaves you with an enhanced admiration for the composer as a thinker and organizer. We all know that Bach was a great man as an artist. He was also great as a craftsman. But you will not realize this except by analysing his craft.

This chapter will be mainly analytical. I expect that makes

you want to skip it! But I'm not going to analyse the whole Prelude for you, only about half of it. The rest, as usual, I shall leave to you to think about.

The first thing to do is to number the bars of your copy. Unfortunately there are two different versions of this Prelude: one, which I like best, is written *alla breve* and has just eight quavers in the first bar's right-hand part. The other version has a mixture of semiquavers and demisemiquavers in that same first bar, and has made two bars of the first version into one. So when I refer to bar-numbers I will have to give you two different sorts: plain numbers, when I mean the *alla breve* version, and numbers in brackets to refer to the second version, which is also that one used by the Associated Board.

The next thing to do is to learn some tunes, and when I say 'learn' I mean learn in your head, not in your fingers. Learn them as if someone had whistled them to you and you wanted to remember them. If you can learn them without playing them at all, so much the better. Sit in an arm-chair and do it. If you cannot do that, you must play each one till you know it in your head and could hum it back.

The first tune to learn is the one which the right hand plays in the first four (two) bars:

Tune A

Example 39

I shall call this Tune A. You will see that it has two nearly similar halves, the second of which ends differently from the first.

In the left hand at the beginning of the piece there is another tune, call it Tune B, which is a counter-melody to Tune A; but it never occurs in the right hand, even when the left hand plays A.

F   81

Tune B

Example 40

Tune C, which begins in bar 5 (3) right hand is the counterpoint to A when A is in the left hand.

Tune C

Example 41

At this point—when you have got these three tunes in your head—I shall pause for a moment to discuss how to learn these tunes as notes as well as sounds. All three, to start with, are in B minor, so get to know sounds/notes of the chord of B minor and then of the chord of the dominant of B minor:

Example 42

I have given you scraps of both chords, written as separate notes, in both bass and treble clefs; also a 'seventh' added to the upward dominant. Try to co-relate all these with the three tunes, so that as you think the sounds you can also think the notes. But think the notes in relation to the key as well as to each other, because later you will meet the same tune as Tune A in another key. For instance, Tune A's first bar revolves round the B, D and F sharp of the B minor chord; and the second bar revolves round the dominant chord, starting with the C sharp going to F sharp. The F sharp then has a kind of wriggle round itself before going on to the rest of the chord, even including

82

the E natural of the 'seventh' at the end of the second bar. The second two bars are nearly the same.

Tune B. Any connection with Tune A can you see? Well, of course, it is in the same key, for one thing; and then it has a 'wriggle' almost identical with the one in Tune A. Otherwise it is a very simple tune to connect with notes.

Tune C: first bar, B minor chord; second bar, dom. seventh chord downwards; and third bar, really a triumphant little downward scale, with one kink in the middle, from F sharp to the keynote and leading note. Notice, by the way, that the first note of each bar of Tune C is one higher in each bar.

I think that it is worth taking a lot of trouble with these simple tunes of the very beginning. Be sure that the *first* thing you do with them is to learn them by ear from memory, then play them so that your fingers get to know them, then analyse them in their keys. You are then exercising your three memories: ear, mind and finger.

We will now go on to the phrases in bars 9–12 (5–6). Learn first this one:

Tune D

Example 43

This is an interesting one because the second half of it is almost a mirror image of the first half. Bars 11–12 (bar 6) is a sequence of the same tunes, one note down the scale. Then learn the left hand part:

Tune E

Example 44

which consists of four straight notes up the scale followed by four straight notes of which the fourth is a jump down to an octave below what it would have landed on if it hadn't jumped down—a favourite jest of Bach's. All this is easy to understand and remember. So are the next four (two) bars which are also in sequence in both hands. Learn the shape very carefully; and when you come on much later to bars 49–52 (25–6) you will find that they are almost the same, but not quite. Find out where the difference lies.

In bar 17 (9) the music returns to Tunes A and B, but this time in D major instead of B minor. You will have to shift your thoughts accordingly, but otherwise it is not difficult to remember. (You will find both these tunes again in bars 41–4 (21–2) but in F sharp minor.) In fact you will probably sigh with relief at meeting your old friends again.

In bar 21 (11) the left hand takes over the D major version of Tune A but the Union of Right Hand Operatives has some grudge against Tune B, so your right hand has new material which again is easy to remember, because it consists of three fragments which all start the same way: (Tune D).

Tune F

Example 45

Then in bar 25 (13) the two hands start Tune A together in E minor. But the right hand gives up fairly soon and does something new while the left hand goes on with the tune. After a run of quick notes the right hand has Tune A in full, and the left hand has the counterpoint which the right hand had in bar 5 (3), but this time the key is E minor and your thinking has to adapt itself to this key, dominant and all, with your old friends, Tunes A and C.

I remember finding bars 33–6 (17–18) very difficult to remember, the first time I tried to memorize this prelude; the reason was that I was clottish enough not to notice that the left-hand part is Tune D which we had before in bars 9–12 (5–6) in a different key; and the right-hand part, which is the one that probably confused me, is really a new tune but one with slight upside-down resemblances to Tune D. I suggest that you learn the left-hand part first and thoroughly here, and don't forget that it is Tune D, even while you are playing both hands. We had better call the right-hand part Tune G:

Tune G

Example 46

Bars 37–40 (19–20) are also difficult to remember and I do not think that I can help you much with them beyond suggesting that the last three (one and a half) bars are based on a diminished seventh chord on B which is going to lead you back to—can you guess and aren't you glad?—Tunes A and B in F sharp minor. Here is the diminished seventh chord:

Example 47

and the two hands are sympathetically syncopated, the syncopations in one hand occurring just when they are not there in the other one.

From now on you have nothing to dread: all is plain sailing, except that the coda in the last four (two) bars has just got to be learned as a thing of its own which has little connection with anything which has gone before. So I will do no more analysing, and how thankful you will be!

But I feel I must say two more short things, one about memorizing in general and one about Bach and this Prelude in particular. In your efforts to memorize, you may find that each hand by itself is fairly easy to remember but that it is the combining of the two hands that is difficult. Combining the two hands is not always just a matter of adding one to the other:

there is something about togetherness which is more than the sum of 1 + 1. So if you find yourself getting stuck, think of the two parts as one thing, one hand balancing the other (as in the syncopations I referred to just now) or some salient note in one hand coming just before or with, or after, a salient note in the other.

Finally, I hope that you will not think, as some people do, that Bach was not an artist because his music is so well organized; that he was more a mathematician than a musician. Nothing of the kind. All great art has to be well organized, because if it were not you would not understand it. You can see this most easily in the great paintings of the world: how one thing balances another, how a line leads your eye to what the painter wants it to be led to, or how the play of light and shadow is arranged to create the most effect. All these things are *planned*. In music the organization is less obvious, because music takes place in time more than in space and involves memory in the listener. In a picture you can see everything almost at once, but in a forty- or fifty-minute symphony you cannot hear everything at once. The creative artist has to plan, whether he creates a symphony, an opera or a novel or a play. But the planning is not the opposite of musical inspiration: it is part of it. So do not think any the less of Bach because he planned so well. It was part of his genius that he did.

CHAPTER 8

Some Scarlatti Jumps

Scarlatti is a good man to study. He wrote hundreds of 'sonatas' which of course are quite different from Mozart or Beethoven sonatas, and almost all of them that I know are lively and interesting and short. Average length not more than two or three pages. But they are quite tricky to play, partly because they were written for a harpsichord and find a modern piano a trifle grandmotherly, and partly because they are full of very quick and sometimes large jumps which have to be done accurately and deftly. In this chapter I shall refer only to a few points of technique in two of the sonatas, and not try to describe or suggest things about the whole of any one.

Let us start with the well-known one in D minor, sometimes called 'Pastorale'. In the Longo edition (Ricordi) it is in vol. IX, No. 413 and starts like this:

Example 48

Number the bars, not counting the first quaver as a bar. In bar 2, the right hand has a trill which should begin on the note above the main note, on G above F. Some pianists think that all trills should be rhythmically worked out and exactly played.

Bars 8–11 need neat playing which becomes difficult if the two hands are too close to each other. I find that if I keep my right elbow a little further away from my body than usual and play the right hand at a corresponding angle to the keyboard I can prevent my right-hand thumb getting entangled with the fingers

Some Scarlatti Jumps

of the left hand. There are many possible ways of fingering these bars. Experiment for yourself to suit your own fingers. But remember that in the middle of a quick passage for both hands at once it is sometimes a help to have a pair of notes played by the same finger of each hand, e.g.:

Example 49

And, talking of fingering, I enjoy my own peculiar fingering of bar 24, right hand:

Example 50

This enables me to finish the rapid demisemiquavers with a rush, which I'm sure is what is needed, and there is time to put the third over the fifth on A. It is quite likely that Scarlatti did this kind of fingering himself. Do not worry about the jump in the middle. The passage goes too fast for bothering about *legato*.

In my concern with fingering I have gone beyond the bars which contain some typical Scarlatti jumps. They are in bars 16–18 (and, of course, in the corresponding place in the second half of the piece), and they concern the left-hand fifth finger, which in most people is the weakest and least competent of all ten fingers. Here is the passage:

Example 51

Some Scarlatti Jumps

There is no very great difficulty about this; in the first two similar bars the fifth finger has to bounce off the F cleanly and land on the C below. As you bounce off the F the whole of the left arm moves slightly in the direction of the next note, only slightly mind, and the hand moves laterally to the left, ahead of the arm until it is over the C, then down. You can practise it, if you like with the fifth finger by itself, from the F to the C. Longo suggests putting fourth on the F. In the third bar you have to jump to the C an octave lower. I find I can judge this easily if I think of the left-hand thumb going to the C above the bottom C, as if I were going to play an octave. But, of course, you do not actually play the thumb at all, you only use it as a positioning finger:

Example 52

In the Sonata in C which starts:

Example 53

you find the same technical problem. But here it is rather worse because there are biggish jumps in both hands almost simultaneously (bars 18–19):

Example 54

The left-hand jump in each bar is the same problem as we had in the D minor Sonata above, but the right-hand jump, a quaver earlier than the left hand in each bar, seems worse because of the thumb crotchet in the right hand and because the effort to cope with it upsets one's concentration on the left hand. In all these jumps the hand must not lose its balance in the air. I used to find that my left hand *did* lose balance while I was worrying about the right hand.

Can you think of two things at once? Of course one can *do* two things at once, so some people might say that one must be able to think of two things at once. But I'm not so sure. It might be that when you do two or more things at once, probably after much practice, your thoughts follow each other so quickly that they seem to be simultaneous. Or it might be that two separate thoughts gradually merge, after constant use, into one thought. In any case, when you have to practise a difficulty such as this one, which involves thinking in two different directions almost at once, I am sure you must at first organize your thoughts deliberately and consciously in a particular order. I use the thumb of each hand to help me both to position each hand and to think of each in the right order. In the following example I put my *thought* chords in brackets, leaving the played notes unbracketed: (memorize the passage)

Example 55

Although these remote notes are played by the fifth, I think more of the position of the thumb in preliminary practice, to get positions right. Eventually, of course, the movement to the fifth must be in one piece. You will see that I do not pay much attention to the right-hand printed crotchet. Unless you have a huge hand (does anyone know what sort of hand Scarlatti had?), you must let it go a little too soon, though of course, when you are used to the passage you must hold it as long as possible. There are plenty of places in Scarlatti's music where absolutely strict time is impossible. It would be reasonable to take a little overtime to do this for instance:

(All left hand)

Example 56   Scarlatti (Longo) IX 442

I want to digress for a minute to enlarge on playing the nearly impossible. We all know the really bad pianist who plays all the difficult passages in a piece too slowly and all the easy passages too fast. His speeds seem to depend on his technical ability. Obviously that is deplorable. But it is unwise to think too far in the opposite direction, that all music should be played in strict time. There must be a backbone of strict time of course, but the living flesh of a piece, so to speak, should have a little 'give' in it, especially in music of the Romantic period. And even in the eighteenth century composers were human, though apparently less sentimental than those of the nineteenth.

Beethoven, who linked two centuries, never cared very much whether his music was easy to play or not, and he said some very rude things to men who complained of its difficulty. But I believe that when he wrote the nearly impossible, he thought of the difficulty as part of the music. He wanted it to sound difficult, part of the struggles of human frailty against truculent material. In the same way, Scarlatti and no doubt some of his contemporaries may have had the same idea, even though their outlooks were very different from those of Beethoven. Scarlatti was at least a great harpsichordist, ahead of his time in playing technique.

CHAPTER 9

Beethoven:
Sonata in C sharp minor, Op. 27 No. 2

I am one of those who find this sonata, the Moonlight, a work of unique beauty, despite its popularity. It is popular partly because it has a romantic title (not given to it by Beethoven) and partly because the first movement is generally thought to be easy to play and the other two movements are very exciting. Probably the 'Juliet' or 'Giulietta' or 'Julie', to whom it is dedicated, was someone with whom Beethoven was deeply in love in 1801, when the sonata was written.

The first movement is pure magic, very soft throughout and 'as impressionistic as anything in Debussy', as Marion Scott says. If you want to play it, you would do well to do four things before you begin: (a) read Beethoven's own instructions carefully, remembering that *senza sordini* means 'without dampers', that is with the use of the sustaining pedal—a gadget not in such constant use in 1801 as it is today; (b) read what Tovey has to say about the sonata in the Associated Board edition; (c) hear two or more different recordings by great artists; and (d) sit down and imagine how you yourself want it to sound. No one should play this movement with the idea that it is easy to rattle off. The technical demands may be moderate: the imaginative ones are very great.

Since Beethoven demands '*sempre pp*' this first movement is a challenge to tone-control within very narrow limits. Even the melody is marked '*pp*' but it must, of course, be a little less *pp* than the accompanying triplets, which are an all-pervasive rhythm and must themselves be interesting and alive, even if they are background music. They should be played with an affectionate and relaxed mind controlling comfortable and fond fingers. The first note of each triplet needs to be gently leaned on so as to give a stress which is greater than those for the other two notes without amounting to an accent. The whole of the first five bars is a mystery, only partially resolved by the untuneful tune in bar 5.

The moment of the entry of the tune needs care. First, the rhythm of the dotted note must be exactly right in proportion to that of the triplet:

Example 57

Though some musicians believe that Beethoven, like Bach, wrote ♫ when he meant ♩ ♪. Some sentimental people make a *rubato* of this moment, not because they really think it ought to sound like that but because their left hand does not get ready soon enough for the chord of bar 6. Hold the previous left-hand chord on the pedal and move the hand in plenty of time to its new position in bar 6, then play the chord at exactly the right moment. All through the movement much depends on this left-hand preparedness for the immediate future. Second, how does one make the tune quite clearly 'the tune'? Part of the art of performance of music, as of a dramatic part by an actor, lies in compelling the attention of the audience to certain specific points. This tune is one of them. But since it is *pp*, you mustn't bang it out: it is better to soften the triplet accompaniment, especially the second and third notes. Play the first right-hand octave at the end of bar 5 with a firm thumb and fifth finger. The fifth finger should be aware of having an important note to play and have a little energy (but not too much) of its own. Relax as soon as it has played, so as to play the following semi-quaver lightly. At the same time, the second and fourth fingers

93

playing part of the triplet must be deliberately gentle. Unless you have a big hand you will want to play all the melody notes with the fifth finger, but it is not hard to change fifth to fourth on the G sharp minim in bar 7, so as to creep smoothly to the A minim just after it. Wherever you have to play two fifth fingers running, release the first one early enough (holding the sound on the pedal) to play the second one in time. Make sure that the two notes of all right-hand octaves sound exactly together.

In bars 15–17 the tune takes on a touch of agony. If you can't stretch to the C natural, this is a place where it is justifiable to play it just after the thumb. This splitting of the ninth can create a sense of tense effort, which I am sure is what Beethoven wanted here. To play the C natural with the left hand is possible but, in my view, wrong. It is too easy. The hairpin cresc. and dim. is no more than a sigh. The first real cresc. comes in bar 25 and the loudest note in the movement is the first bar of 27; but it is not at all a loud loud. In the corresponding place later on, bars 48–9, Beethoven actually marks a *piano* just where you would expect another 'loudest note'. This is typical of his habit of giving you suddenly the unexpected.

In bars 32–5 it is very tempting to grow louder; but don't. A constant *piano* is more mysterious and will heighten the syncopated effect in bar 37 of the crotchet in the middle of a triplet, another of Beethoven's unexpected touches. The crotchet should be marked just enough to give a slight jolt to a listener who has nearly gone to sleep in the previous few bars.

There is nothing new technically in the recapitulation until the coda in the last two lines of the movement, when the left hand has the rhythm of the tune. Again the listener's attention should be forced to notice it, not by a thumping left hand but, as before, by diminishing the other hand.

Tovey has some wise words about the speed of the whole movement. There is no absolute correct speed for anything. What matters here is to play the movement as slowly as you can without giving anyone who listens to you an excuse to say 'how long is this piece going on for'? The time-signature is $\mathbb{C}$ which means that the minim, not the crotchet, is the beat. You may easily play the piece at a different speed on different days, according to your mood. But at its slowest the movement is . . . a movement: it must move.

SECOND MOVEMENT

This is a deft little dance which should follow the first movement without a break. Remember always that it is a dance, and follow Beethoven's slurs and *staccato* marks with great care. Much depends on your being able to hold notes or play *legato* with one part of a hand while another finger plays *staccato*. In the very first phrase, for instance, the tune at the top must be *legato*, but the alto A flat must naturally be detached soon enough to allow you to play the next A flat:

Example 58

A few bars later (bars 9–12) you have to do some neat fingering, with *staccato* and *legato* in the same hand:

Example 59

and there are several places later on where you must do the same kind of thing.

TRIO

Not really difficult if you remember to release those right-hand octaves which precede a jump even though they look like long, non-releasable notes. Every time you miss one of these octaves or feel worried about it, think how you are releasing the one before. The pedal will do all the holding you need while your hands release a long note.

THIRD MOVEMENT

This is a difficult movement but not very difficult. Think of two things particularly: (1) There are only a few loud moments. Much of the movement, rapid and exciting though it is, is soft. (2) The sustaining pedal is used only occasionally. The *staccato* marks, especially in the left hand, really mean *staccato*. If you put down the pedal, the bass does not sound *staccato*. In the general excitement it is easy to plonk down the pedal unconsciously and far too frequently. Don't.

The first technical difficulty comes at the beginning in those rapid broken chords in the right hand. It is not hard to do this quickly:

Example 60

A little harder to do this:

and harder still to do this:

It is important to discover in any difficult passage exactly what the difficulty is, what your hands or fingers do not want to do or cannot do. Here all these semiquavers look much the same on paper, but the playing of them involves all sorts of changes of position. I suggest that you find out for yourself

Beethoven: Sonata in C sharp minor, Op. 27 No. 2

just what those changes are, which you find difficult, and then break up the whole passage into practice sections which will isolate each difficulty and help your fingers, hand and brain (don't forget the brain!) to surmount it. When you have done each one well, then you can practise joining them up. I will not tell you how I would practise the start of this movement. But I will say that in bar 2 (and other similar bars later) your right hand needs a very quick release on the last semiquavers before the quavers, of which only the first is *sf*.

Example 61

The whole forearm must, as it were, take a breath and move to the right before coming down with a smack on the first quaver chord.

In bar 7 everything depends—as I'm sure you will discover—on changing rapidly from the right-hand fifth to first on the C sharps:

Bar 7 (right hand)

Example 62

This is not hard to do, but it will be even easier if you move your right-hand elbow slightly outwards as you play the beginning of bar 7, so as to bring your arm into nice position for the next part of the bar. The substitution of fingers on the C sharps is, of course, done not by the arm force but by quick release of the hand from the first C sharp and equally quick, but light, downwards hand movement on the second one. The music moves far too quickly to do any playing with the arm, though of course you can move the arm laterally to position your hand.

G   97

I remember finding bars 9–13 ridiculously hard and I got to dislike them. But they are not really difficult at all if you (a) maintain a good though slight rotary movement in the right hand, (b) connect in your mind the top notes of the left hand with the lower ones of the right hand, and (c) in bar 13 remember that the left-hand C sharp which is a black note comes with two white notes in the right hand. If you can't stretch the left-hand A natural in bar 10, it is justifiable to play it with the right hand.

Suggested fingering for bar 13:

Example 63

There is nothing technically new in the next few bars, but at the beginning of bar 21, everything changes. The left hand now has a quick rotary movement for its semiquavers and the right hand has a cantabile tune. In bar 21 play the first right-hand minim with a little arm weight—not too much, for it is still *p*—but lighten the arm before you have to play the squiggle in the right hand at the beginning of bar 22. Incidentally, play it on the first beat with the left-hand A sharp, not before it.

Bars 25–8: the right-hand octaves are all hand-*staccato*, but the arm is still the positioning limb. You can move your elbow to get the arm into a playing position as I suggested for bar 7, but here Beethoven considerately gives you a tied note shortly before each moved octave and so enough time to move your thoughts and your elbow:

Example 64

Bars 30 and 32: the right-hand trills are the devil to play. Tovey rightly suggests:

Beethoven: Sonata in C sharp minor, Op. 27 No. 2

Right hand

Example 65

but I should not dream of trying to play them with the fourth and fifth fingers marked in the Associated Board edition. Try the third instead of the fourth. And when you get towards the end of bar 32 lift everything in both hands a moment early, so as to frame your fingers in the air to the shape of the *ff* chord in the next bar. Play it with full arm weight, but make sure that the middle fingers have an energy of their own to sound the middle notes as loudly as the outside ones. Immediately after playing the chord, relax the tension of the hands so as to be neat and mobile with your fingers for the following semiquavers. The same technique is needed for bar 37.

Bar 40: be ready to release the last semiquavers quickly to give you time to play the octave in the next bar; and get your mind and perhaps your elbow ready for each succeeding octave. The last half of bar 42 is a bit hard; why? Because you have to do two biggish jumps at the same moment, one with each hand. If you try to think of both jumps at once you are attempting the impossible; so you must think of one, and prepare it, earlier than the other. I won't insult you by telling you which.

In all jumps which involve moving the whole forearm laterally, think of the elbow as a pivot; and any respectable pivot is static and firm. So make your elbow, while it is being a pivot, static and firm. If you need only to move your forearm, do not let the elbow and the upper arm wander about.

Bars 43–56 inclusive are difficult, though the start is not so bad. But even in the first four bars the left hand has to be particularly alive on each side of the bar-lines, making an extra effort of preparedness for the jump downwards. Difficulties increase from bar 47. It is best, I think, here to keep both hands balanced more or less over the centre of the keyboard and flick

99

the left hand laterally down to its bottom note and back when required. It gets worse at bar 49 because the notes are further apart and you have three notes instead of two in the right hand to play. Practise the jumps as separate exercises, like this:

Example 66

In bars 53–6 it might pay you to memorize the line of the left-hand bass line as a melody, then the chords above it if you can. In the following compressed version of bars 53–4, you will notice that the chords of each hand are the same, though in playing them you sometimes have to approach the same chord from opposite ends, so to speak, with each hand.

Example 67

The whole passage from bar 43 to 50 should be practised slowly at first, but since speed is part of the difficulty practise also fast, but in short fragments, making each fragment overlap a nasty jump. Then practise rather longer sections; and finally the whole passage up to speed. And remember that when your hands have to move by a jump quickly to a new position, they move in a curve. The note you leave initiates an upward bounce of the hand which then moves in a parabola to the new note like this:

Bars 59 and 61–2

Example 68

100

Beethoven: Sonata in C sharp minor, Op. 27 No. 2

If you find difficulty in playing these right-hand split chords, swivel on the middle (second or third) finger after you have played it so that the fifth finger is comfortably in position over the top note, then play it with an active finger. The first two chords illustrated above are technically the same, but the third one is easier because you don't have to swivel much, if at all, as your thumb and fifth are both on black notes. Practise slowly and purposefully at first, but soon your hand will know what to do and be able to play fast, all the little movements merging into one.

After the double bar there is nothing technically new for a long time, and if you have mastered the movement so far you should eventually be able to play the whole of it. Some people find a little difficulty in combining the hands in places where the left-hand phrasing, as in bar 78, goes askew with the regular right hand. This is not so much a physical as a mental difficulty, and the remedy is to be consciously aware of what notes each hand is playing at the askew moment, for instance:

Example 69

Think of the right-hand D coming with the left-hand F sharp at (a) and (b). Finger changes on the left-hand F sharps will give you a free arm. There are several other places with the same difficulty.

In bar 83, 85–6 left hand I found that my hand lost balance when playing the repeated notes. Yours may not; but, if it does, think of a quick hand-release on the *staccato* in each case and a clean start for the next note.

Bars 87, etc.: here your left hand is burbling away with drum-roll semiquavers; no great difficulty about this. But make sure that the rhythm of them is constantly in your ears and that the slower right-hand notes fit in exactly to that rhythm.

Bars 89–91, left hand: keep the rhythm clear by marking the first of each group of four semiquavers with a forearm stab.

From bar 102 begins the recapitulation and there is no technical point that has not occurred earlier. One point, in bars 128–9, raises a general one: when one has a passage requiring thoughtful fingering occurring a second time in a movement, but possibly in a different key the second time, should not one consider *both* occasions together? Bar 128, for instance, corresponds to the earlier bar 34. How do you finger this? It doesn't matter much how you do it, but it will save you time and trouble to do the same fingering if you can for bar 128 as you did in bar 34. Sometimes it is not possible to do the same fingering, but it is always possible to compare two similar places to see if you can. Personally, I do the following fingering because I dislike using a rapid 3, 4, 5 (as some editions suggest):

Example 70

Mind that your hand does not lose its balance as you put the thumb under: practise holding the note before the thumb goes under, just to pin-point it in your mind. Finish the left-hand chord exactly at the rest. The silence in the left hand clarifies the right-hand notes for the listener.

Skip on now to bars 175–6 which contain a difficulty which we have had before, but more of it. You may remember that back in bars 25–8 Beethoven gives you a bit of time to gather your wits together for the big jumps with the right hand; but here he has got a stage further and there is no spare time and still big jumps. If you find bars 175–6 difficult, learn the right-hand melody from memory—it's quite easy to do that—and practise it first with the thumb only, but with the hand stretched out as if you were using the fifth too. It is much harder with the

thumb by itself than with thumb and fifth together, but you get
a good idea of the distances involved this way. Then do it with
first and fifth in octaves, making sure that your forearm moves
enough in each direction to make your playing movements with
the hands easy. Use the second note of the slur (E) as a kick-off
for your jump. Finally, add the left hand and make its semiquavers bind the whole thing together.

The next few bars, 177–83, are rapid right-hand arpeggios in
each direction. Those which go upwards are of course the harder,
because of the 'thumb under' difficulty. The passage goes so
fast that you need not bother about *legato* playing, and it might
be a good thing to practise the upward arpeggios slowly but
staccato, with care that the arm moves upward to carry the
hand (and thumb) upward too. I do not myself find these bars
difficult.

Bar 187: I'm sure Tovey is right in suggesting that one should
'drift downwards from the trill' and without trying to group the
quavers at all. You can, however, group them mentally if you
want to remember them; but don't *play* them in groups. Where
would you start your mental grouping? Mine starts on the first
E after the trill.

If you have practised broken chords with both hands con-
scientiously in your younger days, you won't have any difficulty
in the near-last bars of the piece, 196–8. If you haven't, you
may find them difficult; and it is annoying to have a new difficulty in the last few bars of a long sonata. Well, what *are* the
difficulties? (Have you thought about them or are you waiting
for me to tell you? You will get more from what I tell you, even
in disagreement, if you think before I tell you.)

In bar 196 there is a G sharp for each hand in the first group
of semiquavers. These G sharps come again a moment later, but
here they need 'new' fingers to enable the hands to continue up
the piano. It is as well to be conscious of this. It is a good
principle to isolate a particular difficulty and to practise round
it. In this case I should practise (possibly each hand separately
at first, but of course the difficulty is both together) in this way:

Bar 196

Example 71

Coming downwards, apply the same idea. Do everything slowly at first if your fingers don't want to go into the right places, then faster, then very fast. Think of the arms moving laterally up the piano rather than of hand-stretches to find new positions. In order to make yourself conscious of this, practise the above fragments but add one more note:

Example 72

Naturally, you must use this practising technique for each group upwards in bar 196 and downwards for the next two bars.

I may have described as difficult passages in this great sonata which you find easy, and I have probably omitted to comment on other passages where you could do with guidance. Never mind. Do not rely on me to put up all the signposts. Use your own compass.

CHAPTER 10

Chopin:
Waltz in D flat, Op. 64 No. 1

This waltz is well worth learning because it is an excellent example of Chopin's talent for making pleasurable music with notes which fit the hand. This applies chiefly to the right-hand part, which is much easier to play than it sounds—always a desirable quality for any piece. The left-hand part is an ordinary rapid waltz accompaniment which, once the technique of playing it has been learned, is useful for all quick waltzes.

The piece is sometimes called 'Valse du petit chien' and sometimes the 'Minute Waltz'. I know nothing of the little dog, but I'm quite sure that it is unwise to determine to play the piece in a minute, as difficult a job for most people as the four-minute mile. Even Lipatti, who was a very good Chopin player, took over a minute and a half to play it. It is just a very quick, neat little waltz with pattering quavers, like the dog's feet if you like, in the right hand and a slightly more sentimental middle section. To begin with, I shall discuss each hand separately.

The Right Hand

I suggested in an earlier chapter that rotary movement of the forearm and hand can sometimes be hardly more than an attitude of mind. Here is a case in point. You should not play the quick quavers with the rotary movement, but with the fingers, which can move much more quickly than the forearm. But if you allow the forearm and hand very small rotary movements, the fingers will be unstiffened, and probably in a better position to play. Possibly the rotary movement actually assists the playing movement of the fourth and fifth fingers—though this does not absolve those fingers from doing a bit of work on their own —but whatever you do, do not play the thumb with the rotary efforts: it is quite strong enough to be independent.

The very first bars need very slight weight-transfer movements, as shown by arrows, and personally I prefer the following fingering to avoid contiguous fifth and fourths:

Example 73

Bars 10 and 12 are rather alike, but the twiddles are different. Find out the difference. The first section (36 bars, not counting repeats) is easy to memorize and I recommend memorizing. The middle section I have always found a little harder to remember, but if you can concentrate on the moment in bar 63 where you take a new turn from what you did in bar 48, you should be able to do it.

LEFT HAND

There are two problems as usual: the playing movements and the positioning movements. You will probably agree that in this waltz the chief difficulty is the positioning, that is the jumps. My suggestion is this: that you think of your left hand as being based more or less permanently over the middle of the piano, as in the last two left-hand chords of bar 5 (where the left hand begins), and then when you have to play a single note lower, as on most first beats, your hand swings leftwards, the forearm supporting it and the appropriate finger pointing towards the note until it reaches a point just over the note: then the forearm starts a downward movement continued by the hand further and plays the note, but immediately bounces up

Chopin: Waltz in D flat, Op. 64 No. 1

again so that it can return quickly, still with the arm's support, to the 'base' position.

All this takes a long time to describe and seems complex. But it is, in fact, quick and simple. Two things must be remembered: first, that when you are actually playing the note your arm and hand are more or less in a straight line with each other but *not* straight with the note; and second, that if you want to move quickly from one place to another you must therefore swing your hand in a curve only a short distance above the surface of the keys. You have not time to go in for large graceful, curved movements. Every lateral jump begins with an upward bounce.

Practise these movements the 'wrong' way, three beats at a time beginning with the third beat of each bar and stopping after the second beat, like this:

Example 74

Of the above three examples (a) is easy because you hardly have to move the forearm at all: you just turn the hand a little; (b) here your fifth finger has to go a bit further, so it must move more quickly than in (a) and perhaps your forearm will have to carry it. In (c) you have a long way to go down; your arm is more involved and the pace must be quicker. Don't forget that you have to move up, each time, as well as down; and that you must time your swings each time according to the distance you have to go. The difficulty of all of them is to judge the distance and to play quickly. So do not practise slowly for long, practise short bits quickly and then more quickly. The first beat of each bar must, of course, have a little more tone than either of the others. In fact, one has to play all left-hand notes and chords (with the few obvious exceptions) *staccato*, because one has to move on to the next one quickly.

107

BOTH HANDS TOGETHER

You will find that practising each hand separately does not add up to being able to play both together. You have to practise the togetherness. Listen for this very quality and, if you suspect you are not playing very well, make for yourself definite landmarks where you know two notes that should be together and make sure that they are.

PEDAL

Chopin marked a lift of the sustaining pedal on most third beats. This makes the piece dance as it should. Observe all his other marks too.

CHAPTER 11

Brahms:
Rhapsody in G minor, Op. 79 No. 2

This famous and much-played piece is a splendid example of the more virile side of nineteenth-century music. To play it properly you have to be good at lifting the hands right off the keyboard and, I need hardly say, at putting them down on to the right notes afterwards. Brahms wrote the piece in 1879, by which time the piano had changed from what it had been in Beethoven's day to become what it is today, a big resonant instrument with a rich bass tone and a sustaining pedal that made possible all sorts of effects unknown in the early part of the century. The technique of piano-playing had also greatly developed.

If you want to learn, or possibly re-learn, this rhapsody you should find out what sort of music it is. So try to hear recordings or broadcasts of it, or get a competent pianist to play it to you. When you have done that, sit down and decide, with the copy in front of you, what sort of music it is for you, and how you want to play it. It is important to do this at the start before you get bogged down in technical difficulties, and to do it again when you are half-way through your study of it.

To me, the piece is dominated by the triplet quavers which go almost all through from start to finish with only an occasional pause here and there, and even the pauses contain potential movement. I can imagine a chariot being drawn by a pair of strong and wild horses through a forest. Occasionally, the driver is unsure which way to go and holds the horses in check for a second or two, and then allows them to plunge on their way. You may have quite a different picture or perhaps no picture at all: the music is self-expressive. But I think that we should agree that it has a swinging sweep to it, which never stops.

It is not a very difficult piece to memorize, although the music takes a long time to establish itself in the key of G minor; and I recommend memorizing if you can, for the sake of the sweep of the piece which is easier to keep going if you do not have to read the music all the time.

There is a good deal of arm-swinging to be done here, usually to carry the left hand over the right upwards and downwards. I sometimes think that the technique required to play a piece has a close connection with the character of the music itself, and certainly this piece is a good example: the swings of arm and hand fit in with the surge of the music, even from the very first bar. But what the player has chiefly to think about is that the swings are all different distances and must be judged accordingly. Here are six swings of the left hand only (the left hand goes into the treble clef at times):

Example 75   Molto passionato ma non troppo allegro

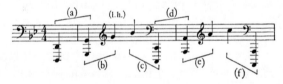

Your left hand, with the arm behind it, will, of course, be poised over the first octave D in the bass at the start. Shake the hand, as it were, out of the arm and play the first chord loudly, but release it at once. The first swing 'a' is only a fourth upwards. Your arm guides the hand this short distance and does not have to move very fast, because it is not far to go. The hand is shaken out again to play the octave G a little more loudly than you played the original D because this G is the first beat of the bar. You must, however, release it quickly and move the arm more quickly this time to guide your finger, the third I expect, to the

110

G two octaves higher. This is swing 'b'. Swing 'c' downwards is a very big one, three octaves from the second finger on the top B flat to the octave C.s below. So you must move very fast. Swing 'd' upwards is not so big, but swing 'e' is two octaves upwards and swing 'f' downwards is the biggest and therefore must be the fastest of the lot, more than three octaves.

If you find these swings difficult—they are not very difficult really—stop and think exactly what you want your hand and arm to do in each case. When you have played an octave low down on the piano, say the first one of swing b, and have to move quickly two octaves upwards what happens to your arm? Does it, (i) move in a graceful curve, slightly up in the air as you release a note and down again when you get to the next one? or (ii) move as straight as possible close to the keys? Does it (iii) move at the same pace all the time? or (iv) get faster as you go on? or (v) slower as you go on? Experiment and see. Of course, you could do the thing in three deliberate movements with a stop in between each: (a) take the hand off the keys when you have played the first octave, (b) move arm sideways until your hand is immediately above the next note to be played, and (c) plonk your hand down to play it. It would be possible to practise like this, but there is an obvious snag. What is the snag? Is there a connection between the rhythm of your arm-swings and the rhythm of the music?

The middle of bar 2 (I number the bars starting with the first complete one) is really difficult, because both your hands have big jumps almost at the same moment—almost, but not quite. Your left hand has a finger playing C in the treble clef and has to jump so that its fifth finger can play A, the bottom note of the piano! Fortunately, it can release its C a fraction of a second before your right hand which has a finger on middle C and a fifth on the F above it, has to jump upwards to the top F. Never try to think of two jumps simultaneously. Even the most advanced schizophrenic would find that difficult. So think of the left-hand one here before the right-hand one.

Apart from that jump, the right-hand part of the first few bars is not difficult, but follow Brahm's stress-marks which point the melody. The melody should always be clear, which means that your right-hand fifth finger in bars 3 and 4 as well as 7 and 8 must do some work on each crotchet, so as to differentiate it from the surrounding quavers.

Bars 8–9

Still no sign of G minor yet! But here is a new musical idea—I don't care whether it is called the second half of the first subject or the beginning of the second subject, what does it matter?—and therefore, a new treatment from the pianist. Hold the last octave beat of bar 8 on the pedal, take the hands off it and get them ready to play the big, resolute chord of bar 9 with full arm weight behind the hand and fingers, the fingers doing some energetic work on the individual notes of the chord. This chord is *staccato* and must be released at once, the hands raised by the arms off the keys and dropped down again with energy, weight and finger vitality on to the next chord. There is nothing difficult about all this, except to maintain energy from wherever you like (in the tummy or is it the brain?) right down to your fingertips. And then you have in bars 9–10 and later:

Bar 9 (left hand)

Example 76

In these pairs of triplet quavers, think of the hand playing the second octave of each pair as a rebound from the first, making a noise like *tudda*, *tudda*, etc. The arm moves upward (up the piano, I mean) in an almost continuous movement; and the hand does the actual playing of the notes. Do not try to play with the arm: the arm is only a positioning limb here. You will find that even more true for the downward octave jumps in bars 12–13, which are rather harder to play. I find that if I think of my left hand making a small curve in the air from the first octave of each pair to the second, I can play it better. Incidentally, the right hand is quite easy, but prepare the shape of every new chord while your hand is in the air, during a rest.

Bar 13—last beat
Do not smudge these right-hand notes with the pedal, but use a finger *legato*. I use on the top notes, 5, 3, 5, but you could use 5, 4, 5.

Bars 14–20, left hand
The chief difficulty here is the positioning of the hand so as to make the passage sound easy and *legato*. But do not try to play the passage with a conscientious finger-*legato*, as you might an ordinary arpeggio: there is no harm in occasionally lifting a finger off a key before you put the next finger down on the next note. On the fourth quaver of the bar, for instance, you will probably want to use your second finger, but you need not strain to put it carefully over the thumb while holding the thumb. You can let the thumb go and move the whole hand up the piano till your second finger is over that F. The reason for not worrying is that the pedal should be down anyhow and will make the passage sound *legato*; and also the notes go fairly fast, so that gaps will not be audible. Think of the whole passage as a series of different hand-positions, as in my extract below. But some of these hand-positions are on the black-key level, others on the white-key one. To get from white to black slide 'in' on the last white-key-level note to the black keys. Similarly, 'out' means slide the hand back, away from the black keys. I have suggested where these slides might occur:

Bar 14 (left hand)

Example 77

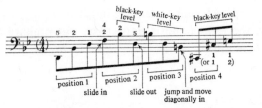

Now apply these principles to the next few bars.

Bars 17–20, right hand
This right-hand part is not difficult. In bar 17 swivel your finger, or rather swivel your hand balancing on your second finger, on the second A in the bar, so as to get ready for the next chord:

Example 78

The same movement is necessary more than once in the next few bars. Of course you have to lift your hand and jump over the barline, as it were, between bars 19 and 20.

Bar 20, etc.
After the loud chord, you need a quickish and real *diminuendo* into the succeeding *mezza voce*. Have you noticed the slight difference, but an important one, between the last beat of bar 20 and the last beat of bar 21? In all these bars the top crotchets must sound a bit firmer than the quavers beneath them: that is why they are crotchets! Of course, you will realize that from bar 21 to bar 32 there is a long crescendo which comes to an angry climax at the double-bar. For the downward arpeggio of

bar 32 I like to keep my wrist low and move my arm down, so that each playing finger feels it has the law behind it. No doubt you will have noticed that there are two sorts of rhythm in these passages:

Bar 27 (also bar 23)

Example 79

con 8

and the left-hand semiquavers do *not* come with any right-hand quavers.

Bars 33–53
The Middle Section. All but one of the first eleven bars of this section involve a swing of the left arm and hand over the right and down again. Remember that the 'down again' is as important and perhaps a little more hard to do than the upward swings, although all swings are in time with the beats and can be rhythmically thought of. It is an enormous help to the player to know this section from memory and consequently to know beforehand intellectually what note each swing is aiming at, especially in those places, like bars 34 (last beat) to 37 (first beat) and the corresponding bars 41–5. In these places the tune is of a different pattern from what it was at the start of the piece, so learn the tune as a tune but with the harmony underneath. Learn it as *sound*. Here is a sort of précis of the passage. Notice that the melody alternates between going down a tone (or semitone) and up a fifth. Your ear will tell you the details if you get the outline in your brain and get reconciled to the fact that the tune is played by each hand, mostly in alternations:

115

Example 80

Bar 40 (and 48)

If you are a little weak on playing 'two against three', here is
your chance to learn it for life. What you have to do, of course,
is to play three quavers of the right hand so that they take up
the same total time as two quavers in the left hand. The right-
hand quavers are triplet ones. Here is how to do it:

1. As you have to play 3 against 2, multiply 3 × 2 and make, if
   your maths are up to it, 6.
2. Think of 6 little beats, but taking up one larger crotchet beat
   of the printed music. As you have in your right hand 3
   printed quavers in that beat, count 2 of your miniature beats
   to each quaver of the right hand and similarly 3 miniature
   beats to each quaver of your left hand, which has only two
   printed quavers. If this is all confusing to you, write it out
   large, so that there is plenty of room to write the beat
   numbers below and see where they occur, like this:

Example 81

4. Play each hand separately and slowly at first, counting the
   appropriate miniature beats.
5. Play both hands together and still count the miniature beats.

Notice that the second left-hand note comes on the fourth miniature beat and the second right-hand note should have come on the third. So you have, I hope, played two notes on two consecutive miniature beats just at this point (but nowhere else). Go as far as the second crotchet beat. After that you merely have to do the same process again. Play all this very slowly at first—you'll have to!

6. Play it a little faster, still counting, but listening to the total sound if you can.

7. Make up for yourself some nonsense syllables which make a noise like the rhythmic sound. Mine are: 'Paté-ee um, paté'.

Some versions of this combination of rhythms naturally have the 2 and 3 in the opposite hands to this version. A nice example in which the threes are in the left hand and the twos in the right hand is Chopin's Waltz in A flat, Op. 42, where the quavers provide the little beats.

There is not very much more which I need discuss in this piece. The two against three business recurs in bars 48 and 52; and in bar 53 one is led to a quiet passage which has a cruel climax in bar 59, made somehow more cruel by the fact that the left-hand quavers do not come with the right-hand ones, and the climax is repeated in bar 62.

I have a particular affection for the long passage which begins so softly and mysteriously at the end of bar 64. The mystery seems to lie in the dotted minim and crotchet chords in both hands rather than in the other notes which surround them. All this leads eventually to the recapitulation where everything except the key is the same as at the beginning. The last two lines of the piece are its coda with a written-out *ritenuto*. Resist any temptation to slow up more than is written out. One does not paint coal black.

117

CHAPTER 12

Debussy:
'Passepied' (Suite Bergamasque)

The first time I heard this piece I thought it was enchanting. I still think so. It is not in the same time as the classical passepieds which you find in eighteenth-century suites, but it has the same delicate gaiety. Debussy was one of the most original of all composers, and this piece is original among his music. I know no other piece like it. And it is not a very difficult piece to play. It does not go very fast. But it has one challenging difficulty: a left-hand part which is mostly *staccato* and must be played lightly and deftly, to keep the dance on its toes. The right hand part is easy.

With this piece, as with all the others I have been discussing in this book, the first thing to do is to become familiar with it as sound: go and buy a recording of it, listen to a broadcast, or get someone to play it to you until you feel the attraction of the music and want to play it yourself. If you are a good sight-reader, try it out for yourself, but imagine what it could be like when you know it well. When you have done that, it is worth spending a lot of time and trouble in thinking and experimenting with the first few left-hand bars at the very beginning, because they contain the difficulty that you will meet all through the piece.

If you balance your hand just above the keys, palm downwards, there are four different movements you can do with it: one, which we discussed in Chapter 10, is called 'rotary' movement, the kind you use to screw up or unscrew something with a screwdriver. You have to use the forearm to do it. Then you can move the hand from left to right in the same plane, moving the hand either towards the fifth finger or towards the thumb. I call this 'lateral' movement. A third possibility is to move the hand with the whole arm forwards, away from your body and towards the lid of the piano or, of course, away from it and towards you. One uses this to climb up to the black-key level or down away from it. And there is, of course, the plain 'up and down' movement towards the keys or away from them. Perhaps I should add a fifth movement, which is not really a hand movement but an arm one, by which you can move your hand from left to right (or the converse) along the keyboard to get a finger into the right position for playing something. This would be a lateral arm movement.

Bars 1 and 2

There are two ways in which to play these bars, according to whether you think of the bass as a pure, unphrased *staccato* or a phrased one. In each bar you have two groups of four quavers. One way is to poise the hand just above the keys and to move your arm, sometimes just your hand, laterally down or up the keyboard till a finger is in position to play, then play with a downward flick of the hand and finger to the appropriate key. In doing this it is a help to imagine, during a group of notes, that your hand is poised over one of them as a kind of base, from which it darts away to play other notes and to which it comes home occasionally. Here are the first two bars, left-hand:

Example 82   Allegretto ma non troppo

In bar 1 you might think of the C sharp as your 'base'; in bar 2, the F sharp. Do all your measuring of distances from these notes.

The second alternative way of playing these bars (and many

subsequent ones) might be called a 'detached-rotary' one. Try it *legato* at first by balancing a finger, probably the second, on the C sharp in the first bar and rotating the hand till the fifth finger can play the bottom F sharp easily and the thumb the top A. Repeat the same kind of action with the next four quavers, and with the two more groups in the next bar with F sharp as your 'base'. In bar 2 you will have to slide on the first A up towards the black-key level for the next notes, and away from the black-key level for the B half-way through bar 2. Then, when you can do this easily and are fairly confident about playing the two bars, do the same thing, *staccato*, as marked. Your hand is now poised over the keys, as in the first method, but allowed to rotate to play the bottom and top notes of each group.

At this point I should like to remind you that the point of this small book is to encourage you to TEACH YOURSELF. So try these various ways of playing these first two bars—and any other ways which seem feasible to you—and find out for yourself what suits you. Everyone's hand is different and everyone has his own deeply ingrained habits of playing, if he has at any time played the piano frequently. So find out which of your habits are still useful and discard ones that seem outworn and useless. Even if you do not succeed in playing perfectly, the mere search for perfection will stand you in good stead.

The technique required for the first two bars will, as I have suggested, help you to play the left-hand part of the next thirty-five bars at least, but there may be one or two small problems en route. One is that you have to keep a steady and almost stiff fifth finger all the time. Never allow it to give way at the knuckle joint or to 'lie down' on a key. Then, of course, you must judge how far away the next finger to the fifth is in any group of four quavers, and how one group joins up with the next. The end of bar 3, for instance, is very close to the first note of bar 4; and the last note of bar 13 and the first note of bar 14 are only one example of two fifth fingers running. It is sometimes worth practising playing several notes with your weakest finger of all, the left-hand fifth. You will have to do it anyhow between bars 59 and 60, 60 and 61, and 62 and 63. My copy has a misprint for the last left-hand note in bar 62. The note should be D. There are also some awkward hops in bar 68 and between 68 and 69. (Bars 36–58, being *legato*, are not difficult to play as far as the left hand is concerned.)

I want now to leave the left-hand problems for a bit and go back to the earlier part of the piece. The right hand has no great difficulties, but you may find the phrasing at the end of bars 15, 16 and 17 awkward to manage. You can leave go *one* of the two crotchets in the last pair but one in each bar, so as to get smoothly to the last pair. You will have to decide which finger to let go, and it may not be the same one each time. But it is cheating to use the pedal, since the left hand is still *staccato* and mustn't sound smudged. The last pair of crotchets in each of these bars is, of course, *staccato*, so lift your hand right off the keys and come down on to the first beat of the next bar with a thud, like an acorn in October dropping from a tree on to the roof of your car.

In bar 24, you have the first of several occasions where you have to play three crotchets in the right hand against four quavers in the left hand. We have discussed in a previous chapter how to cope with two against three, but you may be made despondent at the idea of three against four, which is a little harder though solvable by the same principles. Perhaps you would like to be reminded how to do it.

1. Take the first half-bar and one more note.
2. As you have to play 3 against 4, multiply these two numbers and make 12 miniature beats to take up the half-bar.
3. Count four little beats to each right-hand crotchet, and three little beats to each left-hand quaver. Add another 'one' for your extra beat.
4. If necessary, write out a half-bar plus one more note on a large scale, so as you can see it all on paper, adding beat numbers as below.
5. Play this very complicated puzzle very slowly indeed. Go on

playing it several times. Then get gradually faster and listen to the total sound. Maths first, then sound.

6. Play it up to speed until you can make the sound yourself to some nonsense syllables of your own invention.

7. Last lap: see if you can play bar 40 (or 43) last half, where you have the same problem, but with a rest in the left hand. Here it is on paper:

Bar 24

Example 83

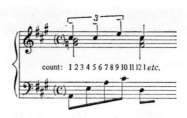

Bar 30 is a horrible one, for the right hand should hold the minim D while you play the two *staccato* octaves. I put second finger on the D and fourth on the F sharp above it. If your hand is too small to play as written you will have to let go the D. It is better to do this than to use the pedal.

There are no new difficulties for some time, but when you get to the delightful new subject in bar 59, you may find it hard to play as you want it. Part of the difficulty is the fifth finger left-hand jump already referred to. I find practising in half-bars a help. Practise up to speed but in short sections and choose your sections to include a difficulty. Bar 68 and its join to 69 are hard, again because of the left hand. Practise in half-bars, each bit ending on the first beat of the next half-bar.

Debussy, or it may have been his publisher Durand, did not apparently want to suggest fingering to players of his piano music, and quite right too! Much better for each pianist to think out the fingering for what are, after all, *his* fingers. The phrasing throughout the piece is very carefully marked and should be a help to fingerers, as is the division of the hands on the last page.

Debussy: 'Passepied' (Suite Bergamasque)

Memorizing

I found this piece rather harder to memorize than most, but a lot can be done to make it easier by discovering the (very logical) design.

Bars 1–2, left hand—are repeated exactly in left hand of bars 3–4.

Bar 3—right-hand tune begins here; first half of it lasts to *bar 6*, at which point the bass of the left hand (that is, the first note of each group of four) begins a step-wise descent of the F sharp mi. scale, C sharp to F sharp. We shall find throughout the piece several instances of step-wise descents.

Bar 7—starts the second half of the main tune, a bit that does not occur again till *bar 107*! Main tune starts again at *bar 11*, but has a new second half, beginning at *bar 15* with a variant of the start of the first half. I was slightly foxed by this, in a memorizing sense, at first, till I discovered that from the end of bar 15 right hand onwards for three more bars there is another step-wise descending line if you forget the leap upwards and treat the top notes as if they were an octave lower, like this:

Example 84

Debussy is obviously rather taken with the upward leap at the very start of the tune, for we get a third version of it at the end of *bar 19* in a phrase which is repeated exactly—all but the last half bar—in the next two bars. The last half-bar was different in *bar 23* because we are now led off to another novelty —the first of the three-against-four cross-rhythms in *bar 24*. Note the sequential crotchet triplets in right hand of *bars 27–9*. Then the main tune begins again in bar 30, rather more robustly and with different harmony—that is one reason for difficult memorizing—and a second half which is nearly the same as it was originally, but not quite. Compare bars 5–9 with bars 34–6. For some reason I could not remember the turn-over of the page at bar 35 till I discovered that the turn-over cancels, as it were, the sharps of B and D in left hand of bar 35. Bars 37–8 are all one chord really; and the old tune starts again at bar 39, but with a difference. Bars 39–40 are repeated in 41–2 and in 138–41, but again with the exception of the last half-bar, because we are again being led to a slightly new idea, an extension of this version if you like. In bar 51 a new fragment begins a four-bar phrase which is repeated a tone lower, bar 55–8. Then the joyous second subject—I think we can call it that here —begins in bar 59.

Let me stop here for a moment and try to pull all this analysis into something helpful. I am sure that the way is to confirm by ear what you have analysed by brain. If, say, you have discovered (or I have discovered for you!) that a four-bar phrase is repeated a tone lower in the next four bars, *play* them several times and listen. Your ear will quickly see the sequence—if an ear can see!—which you have already discovered by looking at the music; so you have at once a cross-check to remembering it. Incidentally, your fingers will have added their bit of muscular memory to it, so that you will have three kinds of memory in action to assist you. But I'm afraid I must stress again that the ear should be your chief memory. Whenever you get into a difficulty, when your brain is muddled and your fingers in knots, try remembering by ear, just the sounds. You probably have no idea how good at remembering sounds your ear is.

So far I have just touched on a few bits of structural design. Obviously I cannot also make a textural analysis of every bar, that is disentangle the harmonic implications of it. And I have no idea how far your grasp of harmony stretches. Perhaps I can assume that you know something about the conventional harmony of the years, say, 1650–1900. In these years, chords were built up in thirds, based on the acoustical overtones of a single note, which started with the third, fifth and seventh. The note C, for instance, felt at home with E and G and even B flat above it. And some composers explored the possibilities of ninths, elevenths and thirteenths.

The Wagner-Strauss period of the nineteenth century was a chromatic one, exploring the semitones between the diatonic notes of scales; but Debussy reacted against this habit and explored instead the effects of adding diatonic notes to ordinary chords, of 'unprepared' and 'unresolved' discords such as sevenths and ninths. Look at this Passepied and observe how few are the accidentals in it compared with, say, Wagner's *Tristan* Prelude; but be prepared to meet ninths and sevenths treated as concords in their own right. For instance:

Example 85

In the above examples I have put in only the essential harmony.

These are, of course, only a few of the interesting chords in the piece. Find out the others for yourself until you feel that you *understand* every bar. This understanding, when allied to the sound, is the path to remembering.

Once you have learned this piece, especially if you have been able to memorize it, you will find other pieces in this suite easy. You will already know by sound if not by finger, the previous piece called *Claire de Lune*. It is still a piece of music worth learning, and if you learn it you will find it easy.

CHAPTER 13

Playing with other Musicians

Few amateur pianists, it seems, take seriously the possibilities of playing with other musicians. I suppose that this is partly due to the fact that all pianists are brought up on a diet of *solo* pieces, like Beethoven sonatas and such like, and are never taught ensemble stuff. Perhaps it is due also to the pianists' illusion that accompanying is a side-line which is either of no interest or else too unrewarding to bother about. But it shows, doesn't it, how lacking in adventurous initiative some pianists are.

Well, I can tell you for a copper-bottomed fact that playing accompaniments or ensemble pieces with other people is just the very thing for amateur pianists. It is also fun of the best kind, for if you do it you will find that the responsibility you under-take towards the other players is a wonderful stimulus to you; that music-making shared with a few other people is five times as enjoyable as doing it by yourself; and, as I have already hinted, that if you ever perform your combined music in public or semi-public, you are not as a rule paralysed with fright, as you probably would be if you were alone. You share the burdens and double the joys.

There are many sorts of ensemble music. The lowest grade, perhaps, is when a pianist who can either read fairly well or else can 'vamp up a few chords' is invited to accompany some partially pickled singer at a smoking concert or a temporarily friendless violinist in the village hall. Usually the pianist gets no rehearsal or hardly any, and he probably gets no applause either, even if he has done miracles of decipherment or improvisa-tion. If you are asked to do this kind of thing and cannot read

126

Playing with other Musicians

fairly well or make up the chords, don't take it on. It may turn out to be a great deal more difficult than you are led to expect.

A much more satisfactory form of playing is when you are asked to accompany a singer or instrumentalist who is willing to rehearse with you and to take the whole thing seriously, though not necessarily solemnly. Gerald Moore, one of the finest accompanists of my generation, has written at least two books about accompanying, one called *The Unashamed Accompanist* (Ascherberg, Hopwood and Crew), a short but very rich book about the art in general, and *Singer and Accompanist* (Methuen) which contains a detailed study of fifty songs and how to accompany them. It would be as impertinent as it would be superfluous for me to try to add anything to what Gerald Moore says. Get hold of the books, read and remember them. But perhaps I may summarize from my own much more limited experience, some of the points about playing with other people, that seem to me worth thinking about.

1. ACCOMPANYING

Do not regard accompanying as an unimportant job, still less as an easy one. To play accompaniments well you must be a goodish pianist and must have, in addition, a willingness and ability to listen to the sounds made by your partner, and to fit in sympathetically your part with his. This means that you should know his part in your head as well as your own; and when your partner is a singer, you should learn the words as well as the melodies of the song, so as to be able to match your pianoforte tone to the exigencies of the poem or the moods of the music, which may be different each verse. Some songs have the same tune for each one of a dozen verses; but nothing is more revealing of the imaginative poverty of a pianist than for him to play all the verses in the same way.

There are two other reasons for the pianist to know the words of songs. One is for him to be able to anticipate in crucial passages the next word which the singer will utter, and fit his accompaniment exactly in time with it. In that famous Handel song *Where'er you walk*, for instance, there are a few silent beats towards the end of a verse and then the singer bursts out with:

Example 86

The pianist should be listening for the 'shshsh' of the singer's 'shall'. Brief though it is, it is long enough at the slow tempo of the song for the pianist to get his big chord plonk with the singer's vowel on 'shall'. The other reason for knowing the words of songs is that, should the singer forget them, the pianist can prompt the singer, sometimes by telepathy (which I'm convinced does happen) and occasionally by a surreptitious mouthing or whisper of the next word. If the words of the song are in a language with which the pianist is not familiar, he can at least discover the general meaning of each verse and the specific meaning of particular and crucial words.

It is obviously a good thing to rehearse with your soloist, be he singer or instrumentalist, as much as you can beforehand. If, as so often happens, the time available for rehearsal is short, try to establish (i) the general tempo of the piece, (ii) any particular places where the soloist wants a special effect, slowing up here or hurrying a bit there or a very definite bit of playing somewhere else. There are, however, some soloists—usually singers, I'm sorry to say—who either do not know or do not care about what special points they are making, or who do not realize that such points, which are so familiar to themselves, are not perfectly obvious to you. As you may never have seen the piece before in your life and have had only thirty seconds' conversation with the soloist probably about what dreadful weather we are having, or how bad the traffic was that morning, it is unreasonable to expect you to know the finer points of interpretation. But some soloists are like that.

Not all, however. My experience is that the better player or singer one's partner is, the more trouble he will take to share his ideas about the piece with you and the more time he will give you to learn them. Personally, I like at least two rehearsals with anyone: one to get the general idea of what is needed, then some time on my own to consolidate this general idea in my own mind and with my own fingers, and finally another rehearsal with the soloist to make sure that what I have practised on my own has been on the right lines, and to add any small nuances of time or tone which we had not, at the first rehearsal, an opportunity of doing.

Whether you are able to have adequate rehearsal or not, you as an accompanist should provide what all soloists need: a basic, definite tempo. At all costs try to agree about this tempo; but if you cannot, at least make sure that it is definite and securely regular. The worse your soloist is, the more he will need your playing to be clear and definite and foreseeable, and any departures from the basic tempo that you do must be done on purpose for a definite reason. Do not, whatever happens, *dither*. It is better to be definite and wrong than dithery and right. If you are definite, you can almost convince the audience that your wrong notes are really the right ones!

If you have had any experience with amateur acting you may be able to detect a very close parallel with accompanying here. The inexperienced actor, when he first tries to act his part, cannot stand still. He will shift his weight from one foot to another, wander about the stage and is never at one particular spot at one particular moment. In fact, he is dithering. As he gets more experienced he learns the value of doing movements on purpose, for some reason, and when he has no reason to move, he stands still. The producer and the other actors always know where he will be at any particular moment. He is a blessing to everyone else, not a curse. The same applies to the accompanist. The soloist wants to know that he will be there, at a definite spot at a definite point of time and not wandering all over the place. That kind of pianist is a blessing—he can be relied upon.

The introductory bars of a piece, especially of songs, may often belong to the pianist. It matters how the pianist plays them. Some pianists—and some soloists, for that matter—do not worry much about the introductory bars. They are there just to give the key and speed to the soloist, they think, or possibly to give the audience time to recover from the beauty of the soloist's dress or face. But the musician has a different view; he knows that the composer wasn't thinking of such things as these, but of the mood of the song or piece. Is it sad? Or calm? Or jubilant? Whatever it is to be, the audience must be lured into the right mood first, before the singer begins. Look at any one of Schubert's six hundred songs, for example, and you will see that this is true. It is also true of many pieces which are not songs, but may have song-like qualities: pieces like Saint-Saëns's *Le Cygne*. Here the pianist must imagine that placid pool with a large and lovely white bird gliding along on it. Then he can begin to play. Otherwise he may create quite the wrong mood.

Balance with your soloist is something to think about. Those pianists who have played for cellists, for instance, may have noticed a certain coolth in the atmosphere after certain passages have been played, and may have wondered why. The reason often is that the pianist has drowned the cellist in places. Cellos have a very large compass, and cellists can be almost as soulful in the middle of the bass clef as when they are soaring towards heaven in the treble one. So the pianist must remember this and see to it that he does nothing to stop this flow of soul. The same can apply, of course, to other artists. The pianist should listen to the quality of every part of his soloist's range and try to judge its power. The low notes of a high voice can easily be drowned. I sometimes wish that the high notes of a high one could be too.

2. PLAYING ENSEMBLE MUSIC

In sonatas for any instrument and piano, in piano trios or piano quartets or in any other kind of ensemble work in which the piano is involved, the pianist's job is not to 'accompany' but to take an equal share of the music and the responsibility for playing it with the other players. You may say—and you would be right—that when you accompany a singer in a serious and difficult song, you have an equal share of responsibility. And it is true that there is no hard and fast line between what is 'accompanying' and what is 'ensemble' playing. But on the whole an accompanist is in the background and an ensemble player is one of a team.

Sonatas for violin and piano form perhaps the largest and most accessible section of ensemble music in which a piano plays a part. Bach, Handel, Mozart, Beethoven, Brahms, Grieg, Franck and Fauré, among others, have written splendid ones. Few of this rich collection are easy to play, but a despondent pianist will find much that is not too difficult in Handel, Mozart and Grieg, and might manage the simpler Beethoven ones and Brahms in A.

If you take on any of these, learn them with as much care as you would a sonata for piano alone, tackling the technical difficulties by yourself so that when you play with your partner you can be free to enjoy the musical problems with him. The fun of these works is the interchange of the chief musical interest and responsibility between the two instruments: at one time you will have to take the lead, at another you will be providing a background accompaniment. This mixture of initiative and self-subordination is splendid musical experience and, I believe, not at all a bad training for ordinary life. The same two qualities are, of course, equally necessary in other ensemble works, trios, quartets, etc.

From a technical point of view, all these works must be practised by the pianist as if they were piano works of some difficulty, as indeed most of them are. But the pianist should be aware of what the other instruments do and should think out problems of balance and ensemble in addition to his own part, and be prepared to listen receptively to the ideas of the violinist or the leader of the group, who will probably have had much more experience of ensemble playing, being a string-player, than the pianist has had.

3. PLAYING FOR CONDUCTED CHOIRS

This is a highly skilled job because the pianist must know his piano-part well enough to give the choir a feeling of complete and constant support, and at the same time he must watch the conductor, do what he wants and generally back him up.

Most choir accompanists have many rehearsals with their choirs and conductors, perhaps once a week all through the winter. By this means they get to know the conductor's foibles, good and bad, and all the places in the music where attention must be particularly concentrated in case the singers wilt or take a wrong turning. But if you happen to be one of those unfortunate brave people who undertakes to accompany a choir at short notice, perhaps as official accompanist at a festival, or as a substitute for someone struck with sudden freezing of the feet, then you must have your wits about you to succeed.

In the first place, you must be a good sight-reader and be familiar with what I have called the 'geography of the keyboard' as with the back of your hand. For you will have to play much of the music with your eyes on the conductor or with at least a side-glance at him, so that you can at least see when he starts and stops, slows down or accelerates. Of course, you will try your level best to have some sort of rehearsal with him and the choir beforehand, or with him alone, if only to learn the pace of the song. Much will depend on what sort of a conductor you are dealing with. There are many competent ones who know what they want and can explain it to you. Unfortunately there are also many of the opposite sort, men or women, who will tell you in a conspiratorial whisper and with a wave of the hand 'it goes like this', only to do something completely different when they and their choir are on the platform.

In such cases and in all other cases of incompetent conducting, the pianist must seize most of the initiative: decide the speed, keep a basic rhythm steadily through the piece, and keep an alert ear for any variation in speed or tone which the choir is so much accustomed to as not to be able to forego. It is usually a good thing for the pianist to learn from memory the first bars of the song and all bars where the piano is alone, taking particular care to know every bar which leads into a choral entry. And remember that a choir of boys' or women's voices needs a firm bass in the accompaniment more than accurate frills in the treble, which they probably will not hear in any case.

4. PLAYING FOR UNCONDUCTED CHOIRS

This is the kind of accompaniment played by a teacher at a school, an organist in a church or chapel, or by someone who is asked to lend a hand to community singing of any kind. In all these cases the pianist is the conductor and the leader as well as the accompanist, and he must take the lead and command the heavenly hosts who are singing.

I well remember the first time I ever took this sort of thing on. I made a complete hash of it. As many other people have made and will make the same sort of hash I will describe what I did in some detail. I was, as it happens, playing an organ in a church; but that makes no difference to the principle of the thing.

There were, I suppose, three or four hundred people in the place all ready to sing a hymn and I had been asked to play for them. I dare say that the word 'accompany' had actually been used, but whether it had or not I was under the impression that I was accompanying. I couldn't have been more wrong. I played the hymn over in the ordinary way and then pulled out a few more stops and plonked down the first chord, loudly. After what seemed to me about ten minutes, but was in fact about a second, the congregation sang the first note. I then put down the second chord, and they took just as long to sing that one. Now, I was under the impression at the time that an accompanist is a modest little man who must always defer to his singer's wishes in the way of pace and time, especially if the singer is in fact, several hundred singers. So I always waited for them to sing one note before I went on to the next. It wouldn't do, I thought, to hustle the poor creatures. The result was that the hymn got slower and slower and *slower*.

Of course, I blamed the singers: how they dragged, I said to the parson afterwards, and he looked at me in a way which can only be described as quizzical, which means an enquiry with a bit of derision in it somewhere. I went home that night feeling horribly uncomfortable, because I knew very well (or that part of my unconscious mind that always tells the truth knew) that it was all my own fault, and that parson had known, blast him! But it made me think.

Of course, any large body of singers will 'drag' if they are accompanied as I accompanied that lot. What they need is to *feel* the rhythm of the hymn or song which they are trying to sing, and the only way in which they can be made to feel it is by hearing it from, believe it or not, the accompanist. So if you have to play for any collection of unison singers who have no conductor, you must play as if you were actually conducting. The only slight difference is that you must give them a wee bit of grace during the very first note since sound travels more slowly than light. But after the first note, play in strict time and the stricter the better. Once they have started they will gladly come with you.

Another point about playing for unison, unconducted choirs, is that you seldom play the printed notes exactly as they are written; and you certainly should never play in exactly the same manner all the way through a song or hymn. Much depends on the sense of the words; a little depends on the size and acoustics of the room or hall in which the singing is done. If you have to play hymns, you may know—if you don't, look at it—Goss's tune to 'Praise, my soul, the King of Heaven', which is in Ancient and Modern as well as Songs of Praise. Goss himself has written three different versions of the same tune, thinking of the organ of course, but the notes can be easily adapted to the piano. Much can be learned from this hymn. In general, variations from the simple printed notes of most hymns can be on the following lines:

(a) For big volume and majestic effects, play the bass in octaves and sometimes the tune in octaves too; but . . .

(b) Once the singers have got going and know the tune, it is not necessary to plug the tune in octaves. What the singers need is a firm bass and harmony in the middle.

(c) For quiet verses or gentle effects, play up in the treble; but you may have to start the verse with a firm bass. Unison singers can feel lost without it: you must judge for yourself as you go along.

(d) Changes of the ordinary harmony make for variety, but don't overdo it.

(e) Short, high counterpoints in the piano part or additional little rhythmic figures can all add something of interest to the tune.

(f) Do not forget the relief to the singers as well as to the player that *rests* give. Also, rests may point the rhythm.

Some examples:

(i) Hymn tune 'Nicaea', usually sung to 'Holy, Holy, Holy'. (See Example 87)

(ii) Last bars of 'My Bonnie'. (See Example 88)

One more point, but a very important one: for any kind of accompanying job or for any job in which the pianist is involved with other musicians, be sure to arrange your piano and the piano stool so that you can easily see the others and be seen by them. Of course, if there is a conductor whom you have to watch, it is essential that you should be able to see him easily.

Example 87

Ho-ly, ho-ly, ho - ly! Mer- ci-ful and might - y!

Example 88

Bring back, bring back, Oh bring back my bon-nie to me.____

This means that your line of sight to the conductor must be as near as possible to your line of sight to the music. If you have a grand piano to play and a conductor raised on a platform, it is usually easy to arrange it so that you can see him over the top of your music. If you have to play an upright piano, you may have to have the conductor a little to one side or in front of you.

If there is no conductor and your accompaniment is the thing that keeps your singers going and, we hope, is an inspiration to them, the singers will prefer to see you. You may even prefer to see them, though a lot of human beings with their mouths wide open is not always a beautiful sight.

All ensemble groups prefer to sit so that their members can see each other. A lift of a bow, the taking of a breath or the

136

raising of an eyebrow may, at any moment, be crucial. Playing music well is quite difficult enough without adding the extra difficulty of partial or complete invisibility to it.

There are many halls and large rooms used for music where the piano, like those who believed in the justice of their cause, has its back to the wall. Sometimes it is an instrument which not only has never been moved since the place was built in 1881, but also would certainly fall to pieces if anyone were to move it now. Never mind: move it! It is worth infuriating the caretaker, the headmaster, the organizer of the concert and, if necessary, the entire Mayor and Corporation to get the piano into the right position and the pianist into a spot where he can see and be seen. If the piano falls to pieces, they'll have to hurry and get a new one. And think how many future gatherings of music-makers in that hall will be grateful!

Index

Page numbers of works to which a whole chapter is devoted are in brackets

Index

Keyboard:
  Geography of, 15
  Shape, 20
  Two levels, 39, 113–14
Kreutzer Sonata, 57

Lateral movement, 57
Lipatti, 105

Matthay, Tobias, 72
Moore, Gerald, 127
Mozart, 43
  Sonatas for Piano:
    In C, K 545, 38
    In G, K 283, 39
My Bonnie, 136

Octaves, 55

Pedal, 56, 108
Pope, Alexander, 48
Posture and Balance, 30–3
Pulse, 27–8

Relaxation, 49
Rhythm, 16–17 (*see also* Cross-Rhythm)
Russell, Bertrand, 61–2

Saint-Saens, 130
Scales, 67–9
Scarlatti (Sonata in D minor, 87–91)
Schumann:
  Album for the Young, 43–4
  Kinderscenen, 77–8
Scott, Marion, 92
Shakespeare, 28
Sonatas for violin and piano, 131

Tchaikovsky, Concerto in B flat minor, 21
Toscanini, 79
Tovey, Donald, 17, 92, 94, 98, 103
Trills, 69
Turek, Rosalyn, 42

Wagner, Prelude to *Tristan*, 79
Weight-transfer, 72, 106

139